ISSUE 19, OCTOBER 2023

AUSTRALIAN FOREIGN AFFAIRS

Contributors

Jacqui Baker is a lecturer in South-East Asian politics at Murdoch University, and a host of the podcast *Talking Indonesia*.

Ryan Cropp is a journalist, historian and the author of *Donald Horne: A Life in the Lucky Country*.

James Curran is the international editor of the *Australian Financial Review* and Professor of Modern History at the University of Sydney.

Yun Jiang is the Australian Institute of International Affairs China Matters Fellow and a former policy adviser in the Australian government.

Sokummono Khan is a Cambodian journalist who films and writes stories for VOA Khmer. She is studying for a master's degree at the University of Queensland.

Phil Orchard is Associate Professor of International Relations at the University of Wollongong and co-director of its Future of Rights Centre.

Margaret Simons is an award-winning journalist and writer. Her most recent book is *Tanya Plibersek: On Her Own Terms*.

Merriden Varrall is a non-resident fellow at the Lowy Institute, where she was formerly Director of the East Asia Program. Prior to that she was a UN diplomat based in Beijing. She has a PhD in Chinese foreign policy.

Australian Foreign Affairs is published three times a year by Australian Foreign Affairs Pty Ltd. Publisher: Morry Schwartz. CEO: Rebecca Costello. Editor-in-chief: Erik Jensen. ISBN 978-1-76064-4260 ISSN 2208-5912 ALL RIGHTS RESERVED. No part of this publication may be reproduced, stored in a retrieval system, or transmitted in any form by any means, electronic, mechanical, photocopying, recording or otherwise, without the prior consent of the publishers. Essays, reviews and correspondence © retained by the authors. Subscriptions – 1 year print & digital auto-renew (3 issues): $49.99 within Australia incl. GST. 1 year print and digital subscription (3 issues): $59.99 within Australia incl. GST. 2 year print & digital (6 issues): $114.99 within Australia incl. GST. 1 year digital only auto-renew: $29.99. Payment may be made by MasterCard, Visa or Amex, or by cheque made out to Schwartz Books Pty Ltd. Payment includes postage and handling. To subscribe, fill out the form inside this issue, subscribe online at www.australianforeignaffairs.com, email subscribe@australianforeignaffairs. com or phone 1800 077 514 / 61 3 9486 0288. Correspondence should be addressed to: The Editor, Australian Foreign Affairs, 22–24 Northumberland Street, Collingwood, VIC, 3066 Australia Phone: 61 3 9486 0288 / Fax: 61 3 9486 0244 Email: enquiries@australianforeignaffairs.com. Editor: Jonathan Pearlman. Deputy Editor: Julian Welch. Associate Editor: Chris Feik. Publicity: Anna Lensky. Design: Peter Long. Production Coordination: Marilyn de Castro. Typesetting: Tristan Main. Cover photograph: UPI/Alamy Live News. Printed in Australia by McPherson's Printing Group.

Editor's Note

THE NEW DOMINO THEORY

Australia has been noticeably candid – even celebratory – about its decision to embark on its biggest military build-up since World War II.

The government has not only released a series of detailed plans about its proposed capabilities, priorities and force structure, but has theatrically announced its major acquisitions, including at a memorable press conference in San Diego in March featuring Prime Minister Anthony Albanese and his AUKUS counterparts – the United States' Joe Biden and the United Kingdom's Rishi Sunak – to announce a "pathway" to providing Australia with nuclear-powered submarines. This build-up has not been a secretive, Manhattan Project–style affair.

Australia's openness about its current military expansion is welcome, and strengthens its calls for others in the region to be less opaque about their own. Yet Australia has been far less explicit about what, exactly, its great military leap forward is for. There has been much talk from successive governments of "strategic competition" and "uncertain times", but little detail about the nature of the actual threat. So, who is the enemy, and why might we need capabilities such as nuclear-powered submarines to confront them?

Of course, Australia has an enemy in mind. It dances around these questions because it is a middle power that wants to avoid inflaming tensions in the region, and because the country against which it might use this hardware is also its largest trading partner.

In the unclassified version of the government's 116-page Defence Strategic Review (DSR), released in April 2023, the lone paragraph about China refers to Beijing's assertion of sovereignty over the South China Sea, its growing reach in the Pacific and its massive military build-up, which is occurring "without transparency or reassurance ... of China's strategic intent". But that is it. These few unadorned sentences hardly seem to justify the theatrics of San Diego.

Three days after the San Diego announcement, Albanese was asked directly by radio broadcaster Neil Mitchell whether he viewed China as a threat. Referring to Paul Keating's denunciation of AUKUS, Mitchell asked: "So he is wrong? I mean, he is wrong to say China is not an issue, not a threat for Australia? Is China a threat? ... Is it a threat to Australia?"

Albanese, in line with the unclassified version of the DSR, avoided offering an answer. He noted China's military expansion and concerns about Beijing's approach to human rights and the South China Sea, adding: "I want good relations. But I want good relations based upon our values and I won't shy away from that. And the truth is that Australia and China have very different political systems and have very different values."

Notably, both the senior Australian figures who have given more detailed descriptions of the China threat have been defence ministers.

In March, the ABC's David Speers interviewed Richard Marles, the current defence minister, and put to him the same questions Mitchell had. "So is China a threat?" Speers asked repeatedly.

Marles gave a different answer, saying Australia needed to protect its trading routes in the South China Sea. He referred to China's naval expansion and its territorial claims, adding: "This is a very big military build-up. And it shapes the strategic landscape in which we live."

Former defence minister Peter Dutton, now the Opposition leader, provided a separate account of the China threat in November 2021, six months before a federal election. Dutton suggested that China was an imperialist power that viewed countries such as Australia as "tributary states". He told the National Press Club that Australia needed to be well armed to be able to defend Taiwan against China, because "if Taiwan is taken, surely the Senkakus [the Japanese-administered Senkaku/ Diaoyu Islands] are next".

These varying accounts of Australia's analysis of the China threat have been evasive, incomplete and inconsistent – a thin guide to the government's foreign policy. The lack of clarity, coupled with the current watertight bipartisanship on national security, has meant there has been little serious public discussion about the reasoning behind some of the most consequential and expensive decisions in recent Australian history.

If we believe we have an enemy, let's name it, and let's try to understand the threat that it might pose.

Jonathan Pearlman

EXCESS BAGGAGE

Is China a genuine
threat to Australia?

James Curran

In 1984, the distinguished historian Geoffrey Blainey – then chair of the Australia–China Council – cast his mind forward to what Australia's relationship with Beijing might look like in twenty-five years. Blainey had noticed the paradox of how, with the Cold War still raging in Europe, Australians tended to employ "double vision" in their attitudes towards the Soviet Union and China. "We close our eyes," he said, "to the suppression of civil liberties and to the iron hand of authority in China, whereas we denounce similar events within the Soviet Union."

Blainey was sceptical that China was a "nation reborn" under the modernising impulse of Deng Xiaoping. He remained pessimistic as to whether the Chinese leadership's embrace of aspects of market capitalism would open up civil society: any blossoming freedom of expression in China, he felt, would find voice in the economic sphere, rather than the political or the cultural. And he predicted tensions in the future over China's repossession of Hong Kong from Britain. It would be a surprise, he said, if, "during the next 25 years, our relations with China are as relaxed as they are today".

By 2009, almost on cue, Australia's official foreboding about China had begun. That year, Labor prime minister Kevin Rudd released a Defence White Paper, its classified version reportedly featuring "blood-curdling" scenarios of how a war over Taiwan might be fought, with an "explicit discussion of the Chinese military threat" that included "missile strikes, port blockades [and] submarine warfare". Around this time, Rudd also remarked to US secretary of state Hillary Clinton that countries needed a "Plan B" for China, "preparing to deploy force if everything goes wrong".

This was a world far removed from Bob Hawke's vision of Australia–China relations as a "model" for how societies with different political systems might get along. Blainey clearly did not buy into that. The high point of Australian engagement with China in the 1980s arrived in what the historian argued was a "freak phase of our history". He could not remember a preceding decade in which the country had felt so secure. "Since the early 1970s, a calm has descended, a calm almost unique in our history," he observed, "and our cordial relations with China are a crucial cause of that calm."

Blainey had a point. From the middle of the nineteenth century, when first the European empires jostled for territory in the Pacific, only rarely have Australian policymakers been able to take a sabbatical from strategic anxiety. From the 1890s to World War II, Japan was the standard bearer for the Asian menace; following the realisation of those fears in 1942, it took until the middle of the following decade for Australian ministers and officials to drop their concerns that Japan might one day rearm. During the 1950s and 1960s, fear of Indonesian political instability made it, too, a state of suspicion, with disagreements between Canberra and Jakarta over West New Guinea a festering sore in the relationship; the mutual mistrust reopened over Sukarno's policy of "confrontation" towards the new Malaysian Federation. That suspicion of Indonesia, brought into sharp focus by its forceful annexation of East Timor in 1975, was only broken by the signing of the Keating–Suharto agreement for maintaining security two decades later. And of course China, which had roused colonial hysteria back in the 1880s, had returned at the height of the Cold War as the "red peril", the source of all regional insurgencies. Meeting the "downwards thrust" of communist China in South Vietnam sanctified the Australian–US alliance.

The end of the Cold War brought a decade of relative strategic calm to the region, yet Australian faith in the need for American primacy survived. Many Australian policymakers believed it would never end. Some still believe it never will. But from the turn of the century, the United States was bogged down in the Middle East, and China became more brashly confident following the 2008 global financial crisis. Concerns about a rich China spending more on its military intensified. As the limits of US power were brutally exposed in Afghanistan and Iraq, China began to show how it might extend its strategic reach.

Xi Jinping's new nationalism returned Australia's outlook to situation normal – that is to say, strategic anxiety. From around 2016, the Australian public has been subjected to a concerted attempt by political leaders and a compliant media to prepare for possible war with China. It has worked. The latest Lowy Institute poll found that, just as in 2022, some 75 per cent of Australians believe China will pose a military threat to Australia within the next two decades. Even though the recent Defence Strategic Review pointed to "the remote possibility of any power contemplating an invasion of our continent", it added that "the threat of the use of military force or coercion against Australia does not require invasion".

The "China threat" narrative is hardening into dogma

According to the Albanese Labor government, the protection of trade and supply routes in the South China Sea and the Strait of Malacca now requires Australia to meet the threat from China further from its shores. Cyberwarfare and long-range precision missiles, too, have shattered the nation's geographical buffer. Blainey's prediction of future trouble with China was accurate, but his totemic "tyranny of distance" now offers no comfort to defence planners. They meet the future by going back to the past – refitting the old Cold War policy of "forward defence" to keep the threat from Asia as far away as possible.

But the question is whether the assumption guiding current policy is correct. Is China not merely a source of unease but a genuine threat to Australia?

The strategic air in Australia has for many years now resounded with the thumping talk of imminent conflict. The "China threat" narrative is hardening into dogma. But how likely is war with China, given Beijing's ongoing need for growth – to ensure its internal stability and therefore the Chinese Communist Party's control – and its continuing hunger for Australia's natural resources?

These are difficult questions, but they must be addressed publicly, especially by our policymakers. How else is the broader community, which is largely uninterested in foreign and defence policy outside of times of war, expected to navigate between the sensationalist portrayals of the "China threat" in media commentary and political rhetoric, and the task of being legitimately concerned about China's ultimate intentions for the region and for Australia?

What are China's intentions?

Well might there be public and political unease with Xi Jinping's China. The worry is not so much of countries falling like ninepins before the advancing tide of the People's Liberation Army: China is not about to march its troops across Asian borders. Rather, it is of states succumbing to China's influence and finding themselves powerless to push back. As the Brookings Institution's Ryan Hass observes, Beijing "works hard to feed this perception of itself as the resident rising power". The suite of its strategic and economic activity has reinforced the basic premise of Chinese ascendancy.

These include China's island-grabbing in the South China Sea, its Belt and Road Initiative, the work of its Asian Infrastructure Investment Bank, Xi's active selling of a "China model" as a guide for developing countries, its diplomacy in the Pacific, Middle East and Central Asia, and its increasingly bellicose sabre-rattling over Taiwan. The war in Ukraine has only intensified this noise in Western capitals, and not just because China, having long championed the need for international respect of its territorial integrity, refuses to condemn the illegal Russian invasion and continues to nurture its relations with Vladimir Putin's Kremlin. Rather, the Ukraine War is seen as having critical consequences for Taiwan: either as a spur for Xi to take action while the West is focused on Europe or as a warning to Xi about the West's capacity to inflict economic – or, ultimately, military – pain on any act of aggression.

It is not hard to understand why this perception of China's strategic activity has evolved, even if President Joe Biden and Secretary of State Antony Blinken are rightly at pains to refute the idea that there is a "new Cold War". Xi's speeches brandish their own hostility and intimidation – over what he sees as an ailing Western democratic model, over Taiwan and indeed towards any country seen to be resisting China's belief that its time in the sun has come. China's image in North America, Europe, Japan, South Korea and Australia is now fixed: as a power looking for national rejuvenation and atonement for the "century of humiliation" it suffered at the hands of Western powers, and willing to bully to get its own way and economically coerce other countries. Its "wolf warrior" diplomacy has only further inflamed concerns about its intentions. Xi's authoritarian grip at home and the urgency with which he talks about taking Taiwan has convinced many across the globe that war is coming, and soon.

The Albanese government has been careful and assiduous in its rhetoric of "stabilising" relations with China. But some observers clearly wish to remind the public and policymakers of what remains at stake. In March 2023 a series in *The Sydney Morning Herald* and *The Age* titled "Red Alert" presented the spectre of Beijing's missiles raining down on Australian beaches within seventy-two hours of a conflict unfolding in the Taiwan Strait. Neither Albanese nor his ministers bang the drums of war, but their assumptions about the strategic environment replicate those of their predecessors. Against the backdrop of China's military build-up and modernisation, government ministers repeatedly stress that the circumstances they face are unlike anything since World War II. The word "statecraft" has breezed into the foreign policy lexicon like an old guest welcomed back from the diplomatic grand balls in nineteenth-century Vienna. But it cannot mask that Labor is committed, at least in its rhetoric, to muscling up militarily.

A range of former political leaders, ambassadors and others have repudiated the argument that China constitutes a genuine threat to Australia. The most forceful response has come from former prime minister Paul Keating. At the National Press Club in March 2023, Keating asserted that:

the only way the Chinese could threaten Australia or attack it is by land. That is, they bring an armada of troop ships with a massive army to occupy us. This is not possible for the Chinese to do because you would need an armada of troop ships, and they'd need to come 13 days of steaming 8000 kilometres between Beijing or Shanghai and Brisbane, say. In which case we would just sink them all.

Keating's bluntness revealed how the China debate in Australia since 2017 has tended to skirt this straight military depiction of the "threat" in favour of arguments about, and indeed evidence of, Chinese interference and regional destabilisation. Put plainly, he was underlining the absurdity of revisiting the invasion scare scenarios that haunted Australians' thinking about the world in the late nineteenth and early twentieth centuries.

For many years, getting to the bottom of China's intentions towards Australia invited two answers. The first: that China's aim was to peel Australia away from the American/Asian alliance system, a view expressed by the author of the US "pivot" to Asia, Kurt Campbell, now President Biden's regional policy "tsar" and the chief architect of the AUKUS agreement. In July 2023 Campbell spoke publicly of a certain anxiety in Washington "not very many years ago" that Australia had "flirted" with a "different set of strategic circumstances", clearly implying that some in US officialdom believed Australia was about to drift permanently into China's orbit. Yet the alliance's history since the late 1990s, in which successive governments have tightened the military, logistical and emotional bonds of the American embrace, sit oddly with such a claim. If China believed that its profitable trading relations with Australia would eventually see Canberra move under its sway, that was a fundamental misreading of the sentimental, cultural and historical roots of the Australian–American alliance. In any case, Campbell answered his own question when he remarked privately in Europe in 2022 that AUKUS "gets Australia off the fence and locks it in for the next forty years". The remark was not far removed from a comment made in 2017 by Ely Ratner – now head of Asia policy at the Pentagon – that Australia was an exemplary ally of the United States everywhere around the world … "except in Asia".

The second response to whether China had malign intentions towards Australia was to state that its internal dilemmas acted as a brake on any predatory behaviour abroad. In this reading, China's ambitions were limited by its ageing population, its internal environmental challenges and the Communist Party's preoccupation with maintaining control – in part by ensuring ongoing prosperity and the expansion of China's middle class. A more sophisticated reading of China's intentions was offered by Geoff Raby in *China's Grand Strategy and Australia's Future in the New Global Order* (2020). A former Australian ambassador to China, Raby argued that far from posing an existential threat to Australian security and prosperity, Beijing is akin to "Prometheus Bound", a great power facing constraints imposed by history, geography, resource reliance and poorly executed soft power.

As Raby pointed out, Beijing has unresolved territorial issues with India, Myanmar, North Korea, Pakistan, Russia and, in the South China Sea, Vietnam. It is also "pinned down by the weight of the Qing Dynasty's imperial ambitions" in Xinjiang and Tibet. In Taiwan and Hong Kong, its strategic options narrow as critical demographic and cultural trends also move in the wrong direction. China's resource and energy dependency, too, Raby suggests, would have had some in the Zhongnanhai waking up in the middle of the night in the mid-2000s and "screaming into the ceiling 'What have we done?'". Lastly, Chinese soft power, tightly tethered to the party narrative, has clearly failed to arrest a sharp decline in Western public opinion towards China.

China's rise has stirred once more the United States' sense of mission and national destiny

Yet there remains the recent record of Chinese economic coercion against Australia, and no doubt the growing conviction in Beijing that Australia is working with the United States to contain it, especially through the AUKUS agreement and membership of the Quad. Arguments will rage for years over the cause of the import restrictions China placed on Australian wine, barley, coal and other goods. Public provocations flung at, by and between the respective capitals hardly helped matters. In any case, Beijing declared its hand: while it continued to trade profitably with Australia in valuable resources, it did not hesitate to punish Canberra and freeze diplomatic contact at the highest levels.

Some of these restrictions on exports are now being eased, but whether they justified the extent of anxiety about the China "threat" is arguable: most of the industries affected, with the exception of wine, were able to diversify into new markets. Nevertheless, the point remains that China was out to weaponise trade to try to gain concessions from Australia, and to make it pay for "pushing back" against Beijing. Even when all the trade restrictions are dropped, the legacy of this episode will continue to undermine political and public confidence in its intentions. Those attitudes will take a long time to shift.

America and the Taiwan trigger

Australia's fears of China should not be sourced solely to its particular geopolitical circumstances or historical memories. They are profoundly shaped by what is being said and discussed in Washington. As in Australia, US policymakers dread the consequences of Beijing's rising power. But the American debate has an extra edge: China's rise has stirred once more the United States' sense of mission and national destiny.

Since the presidency of Barack Obama, successive American leaders have marshalled various wagons in an attempt to keep China in check – first through a US "pivot" to Asia, then through Donald Trump's trade war, and now with President Biden's *CHIPS Act*. The primary fear is that China will attempt to displace America from its position of primacy in Asia, which is deemed by many in Washington as an existential threat. And so the anti-China rhetoric only escalates, even if there are occasional attempts – notably by Treasury Secretary Janet Yellen and National

Security Advisor Jake Sullivan – to maintain some areas of cooperation. Witness Biden's abandonment of "strategic ambiguity" on Taiwan on no fewer than four occasions. Those remarks were dutifully walked back by his staff, but much of the talk of goodwill and "guardrails" has fallen by the wayside, leaving officials scrambling to maintain dialogue.

Beijing's belligerent response to then House Speaker Nancy Pelosi's visit to Taipei in August 2022, and her Republican successor Kevin McCarthy's meeting with the Taiwanese president in the United States in April this year, have increased the temperature in US–China relations. And while the US now talks of "de-risking" rather than "decoupling" economic ties with Beijing, it has taken steps to try to cripple China's capacity to achieve a breakthrough in semiconductor technology, critical for industry and arms leadership. With the Biden administration's elevation of the Quad to the centre of its Asia policy, the AUKUS announcement in San Diego in March 2023, Japan's increase in defence spending, and agitation by hawks in Tokyo for the country to break with its pacifist constitution, Beijing cries containment. Even the recent Korea–Japan rapprochement, while centred on their joint fear of North Korea's nuclear capabilities, has a clear China dimension. But as historian Neville Meaney asked in 2011, "would the hubris of super power nationalism tempt China to take great risks? Would it replicate the irrationality and fanaticism of the Japanese in the Pacific war?" The possibility that such a confrontation might escalate to a nuclear war, added Meaney, remains the "greatest deterrent to such aggressive actions".

The orthodox view of the debate in Washington is that the "China threat" is the only glue holding a fractured and dysfunctional American polity together. The fact that American military chiefs give themselves the licence to predict timelines for a Chinese attack only adds to a prevailing mood of inevitability about war. CIA director William Burns reminded one audience in February that President Xi had ordered China's military to be "ready by 2027 to conduct a successful invasion of Taiwan".

But, writing in *Foreign Affairs*, international relations scholar Jessica Chen Weiss has warned of alarm over a Chinese invasion becoming a self-fulfilling prophecy. She argues that "such fears appear to be driven more by Washington's assessments of its own military vulnerabilities than by Beijing's risk-reward calculus". Against Xi's rhetoric of 2021 that Beijing would take "decisive measures" if provoked, Chen Weiss points out that the CCP reiterated in 2022 that "peaceful reunification" is its "first choice". It is important to remember, too, that Taiwanese visitors to China are accorded many of the privileges of Chinese status, and a higher status than those from Hong Kong. China will clearly not disavow the use of violence, but mediation remains its preference. Even Matt Pottinger, President Trump's former deputy national security adviser, concedes that US–China conflict over Taiwan "is not certain or imminent". And reporting by *Nikkei Asia* in 2023 detailed how the CCP, uncharacteristically, has allowed debates on social media to highlight how unrealistic and dangerous it would be for China to forcibly unify with Taiwan.

This alternative reading of China's actions is rarely heard: that Beijing's bellicose rhetoric and responses to provocations like the Pelosi visit are designed expressly to avoid war. Of course, China's show of military might opens up the risk of accident or miscalculation, and they clearly are an attempt to ensure others stick to the status quo. But it is also clear that, at every stage, Beijing has insisted it wants the Taiwanese leadership to keep well away from red lines. So rather than presaging war, these actions might be seen as helping to maintain the peace. Taiwan understands this too, and it is doubtful that, outside the election of an extreme candidate as president – not an impossible scenario – Taiwanese elites are looking to bring on conflict with China.

The soaring rhetoric of the alliance is at odds with the reality

For the more aggressively nationalist wing of the US Republican party, though, such a reading should be brushed aside. Instead, they believe that the US should bring on the conflict. Two senior figures in the Trump administration – former secretary of state Mike Pompeo and former national security advisor John Bolton – appear to want America to act while it has the military advantage. Both have suggested their party take to the next presidential election the policy of recognising an independent Taiwan. The other scenario, of course, is that Chinese military weight will be greater, prompting the United States to depart the field or choose not to fight – a possibility Hugh White has consistently raised.

Australia: Big ambitions, old ideas

It is doubtful that an Australian government of either political stripe would use its influence in Washington to excuse itself from any conflict. What the Albanese Labor government will never say is that Australia's purchase of nuclear-powered submarines make it virtually impossible for Canberra to say no to Washington in the event of war with China in East Asia. The government maintains it will have sovereign control over its projected fleet of nuclear-powered submarines, but the reality is that the new capability, if and when delivered, will form a relatively small addition to the Americans' Indo-Pacific fleet. Australia's capacity for independent decision-making is therefore limited. As former prime ministers Robert Menzies and Harold Holt showed in framing Australia's military contribution to the war in Vietnam, this kind of commitment is entirely in keeping with the Australian tradition of alliance maintenance.

Australia is now trapped between two instincts that have been historically conditioned: fear for its national survival and the imperative of loyalty to its great-power protector in Washington. The soaring rhetoric of the alliance is at odds with the reality that, for the foreseeable future, Canberra will only be able to contribute what it has historically been able to: a niche military commitment to an American-led war. A revealing comment published in *The Australian* by foreign editor Greg Sheridan in April 2023 suggested that this was in line with the policy settings employed by previous governments:

Serious people who have been at the heart of national security [say] that really the defence establishment doesn't want any Australian government ever to have a serious war-fighting capability. At the end of the day, they think, the Americans will determine everything, they will succeed or fail, there's nothing we can do beyond local policing, basing some American equipment here and symbolic deployments to show the Americans we are really good allies.

That sounds very much in the same vein as the niche Australian deployments contributed in Vietnam, Afghanistan and both Gulf wars. If so, Canberra has a credibility problem. The Albanese government is wary of being seen to commit too much funding to defence at a time when the economy faces substantial cost-of-living pressures and budgetary strain. And that means a gap between the strategic judgement of an imminent threat posed by China – often couched in the language that the "warning" time of any conflict has dramatically shortened – and the long time lag in Australia's acquisition of a meaningful defence capability, both as an auxiliary of the United States in any war and to adequately defend the Australian continent and help armour the archipelago to its north.

Australia's strategic policy, therefore, is a chronological mess. It has the stopwatch beginning its unforgiving countdown at the very same time as it coddles old Father Time.

So what can Australia do? Is the Albanese government playing a waiting game, perhaps privately doubtful that the nuclear-powered submarines will be forthcoming from the United States? A future American administration might be concerned about technology security, or might come to the view that it needs to keep the promised Virginia-class submarines for its own purposes, the latter view already being heard from senior Republicans in Congress. And then there is the cost. There is a possibility that the government's rhetoric on AUKUS is empty. Nevertheless, all the emphasis from Albanese and Marles is in the opposite direction. They are AUKUS true believers.

But this again underlines the discordance between Australia's rhetoric and its actions. Government speeches focus on the pressing needs of the country as it faces its most dramatic international circumstances since the end of World War II – a judgement fuelled by its strategic anxiety and fear of China. Yet, curiously, it has not included funding for the recommendations of its own Defence Strategic Review in the forward estimates. The government talks a big game, but the fiscal muscle to realise its defence policy of "impactful projection" remains missing.

China charm?

The question of the China threat becomes more complicated in an era in which President Xi – as he put it in June 2021 – wants to make China "loveable and respectable". China has done an about face on COVID lockdowns, on controls on big tech firms and the property sector, and on wolf warrior diplomacy. These moves demonstrate China's capacity for swift policy change. The Asia Society's Neil Thomas has recently noted that Chinese policymaking is "becoming increasingly volatile, as China's mounting challenges lead Beijing into deeper swings between the politics of its ideological agenda and the pragmatism of delivering a baseline of economic growth". Abroad, its overwhelming desire is to rescue its international image, and especially its relations with members of the European Union. To be sure, Beijing also wants to prevent Russia's defeat in Ukraine, and hopes to see NATO and the US alliance slip into disagreement, along with ongoing disillusion in the United States itself.

Canberra has no option but to continually weigh the nature of the China threat

The Chinese response to the AUKUS announcement in San Diego, and to the release of the Defence Strategic Review, has been relatively muted, suggesting it is not too perturbed. Certainly, Beijing would not see Australia's relatively modest commitment as in any way changing the strategic balance a decade or more from now.

From Australia's Defence Strategic Review, China will grasp that the actual increase in "deterrence" of a Taiwan adventure is small. But the implied threat, unmentioned in the publication, is that in the event of a military conflict, an "interchangeable" US ally in Canberra means for Beijing the closure of Australian iron ore and other resources and agricultural trade. Such a devastating blow to Australia's economy is never mentioned in these strategic reviews – economics and national security remain in uncooperating silos.

Nevertheless, great caution must be exercised in assessing Beijing's charm offensive. As former Singaporean Ministry of Foreign Affairs head Bilahari Kausikan has observed, it would be a mistake to believe that Xi's institution of emergency domestic measures equates to a reassessment of his strategic policy. That said, Kausikan does not see conflict around the corner. "No Chinese leader," he argues, "will survive a botched or failed war over Taiwan."

What can Australia do?

Like any prudent government whose first duty is the protection of the nation, Canberra has no option but to continually weigh the nature of the China threat. To date, one of the government's answers to this problem is to pursue what foreign minister Penny Wong calls "regional strategic equilibrium". This framework is grounded in the idea that Australia's best defence lies in the "collective security of the Indo-Pacific" – which appears to presume the region will arrive at multipolarity sooner than may be the case, and that Asia will transcend the US–China binary and come to resemble a concert of power.

But "collective security" can only work if the respective states, and particularly the great powers, can put aside their national interests. That is, these powers must have sufficient confidence in each other to act for an agreed common good, regardless of how it might affect their own people, ideology or interests. Neither under the League of Nations nor under the United Nations – the two institutional expressions of "collective security" – have these conditions obtained. Indeed, the "realist school" of international relations has argued that "collective security" is an illusory idea, which, if it were taken seriously by any great power, would be its own undoing.

The policy options open to Canberra, in a climate of persistent anxiety over China's intentions and given the deeply enshrined faiths of the American alliance, are difficult. For the moment, Wong's strategy is to ensure coalitions such as AUKUS and the Quad work "alongside ASEAN and other regional architecture to advance our shared interests with the countries of Southeast Asia". Wong wants, ideally, Australia's relationship with Washington and its regional engagement to be mutually reinforcing. This comes up against the persistence of US–China strategic competition. Attempting to burnish her credentials in South-East Asian eyes, Wong presses the Americans to do more to reduce the risk of conflict with China and make economic engagement a "core alliance priority". Her remarks reflect the reality that America's Asian economic footprint remains patchy. Its "Indo-Pacific Economic Framework" is a start, but its denial of market access for South-East Asian partners rankles. And there is continued disquiet over Washington's absence – unlikely to be reversed anytime soon – from the region's bigger multilateral trade arrangements. Conscious of South-East Asian countries' longstanding distaste for being a staging ground for great-power rivalry, Wong stressed that Canberra is "meeting the region where it is".

The message is significant since South-East Asian capitals have consistently said they do not wish to become pawns in US–China strategic competition. The problem is that South-East Asian capitals are likewise entitled to meet Australia "where it is", and they see an Australia locked into the task of preserving American strategic primacy.

Canberra should therefore pursue a regional economic-based agreement that embraces military, climate, food and energy security, and that might be crafted around existing institutions. It is already working with Indonesia to give tangible and meaningful content to the ASEAN outlook on the Indo-Pacific, deploying ASEAN-centred arrangements to strengthen regional cooperation, stability and prosperity. This is part of a renewed discussion in South-East Asia about "comprehensive regional security", an exchange which begins with the premise that neither the bifurcation of Asia nor its dominance by a single power are palatable for the vast majority of states in the region. Such ideas could be influential in the short term if Xi feels aggression against Taiwan is too dangerous.

Australian policymakers should also watch Japan and Korea intently – after all, they have more to lose if the United States is unreliable or if war breaks out. Another priority is to maintain a close eye on Australian trade with China. Any Chinese moves towards decoupling would be troubling, given China's importance to Australian economic prosperity. Albanese is fond of reminding the Canberra press gallery that Australia's trade with China is "more than the trade combined with the US, Japan and South Korea". This important reminder went missing during the prime ministership of Scott Morrison. In the meantime,

Canberra must pursue the status quo in Taiwan more aggressively. After all, the Kuomintang party might provide the next Taiwanese president.

All of this underlines the need in Australia for a thorough, balanced discussion of the "China threat". The Morrison and Albanese governments have struggled to articulate a compelling case to the Australian people about the nature of the threat and the defence capabilities needed to confront it. Indeed, the entire edifice of current Australian strategic policy is founded on a largely unstated, untested and purported "threat".

The lack of political leadership on this question has allowed the media and some of the more vocal in think tanks to stoke the contemporary debate with fear and loathing, often in Churchillian terms and trapped in the emotional straitjacket of the Cold War. Such a debate should not rely on obsessions with China's posturing or past historical analogies, which are often poorly understood. It must focus on what China can really do and achieve. And it must ask the question about what Australia's role should be – as a responsible, not acquiescent, US ally, and as a middle power that is seriously engaged in forging comprehensive security in the region of which it is a part. ∎

SHAKY GROUND

Are we getting China right?

Merriden Varrall

It's not radical to observe that what China does in the world provokes considerable interest. A lot of the abundant commentary on China talks about its growing "muscularity" or "assertiveness", or its leaders' "strongman tactics" or "wolf warrior diplomacy". The image that emerges is of a China that is confident to the point of arrogance, and increasingly unafraid to "shirtfront" its way to achieving its interests.

Accordingly, the conventional wisdom in the United States and Australia, and increasingly in Canada and in many parts of Europe, is that China is a "challenge" that needs to be managed. For the most part, the appropriate response involves some combination of containment and deterrence, such that any debates are now just about how to get those aspects right. But is this discourse sufficiently nuanced? Or are we missing something important that risks driving a further downward trajectory in Chinese–Western relations, with the potential for consequences that would be catastrophic – as well as tragic, because they might be avoidable?

In this article, I'd like to shift the focus away from questions of *what* China is doing, and instead ask *why*. Why is China doing what it's doing in its foreign policy? Understanding why China acts is crucial to creating effective responses. I should acknowledge that I have had no chance to enjoy frank discussions with President Xi or any member of the Politburo Standing Committee about China's foreign policy. But then, as far as I know, neither has anyone else who purports to explain what China wants. For this exploration, I have drawn on publicly available literature, fifteen conversations with experienced China watchers of various sorts, including current and former political actors, diplomats, academics and businesspeople (many of whom have decades of experience living and working in and with China), and my own research and experience working on Chinese foreign policy.

Putting aside the use of the word "enemy", it is worth recalling Sun Tzu's statement in *The Art of War*: "If you know the enemy and know yourself, you need not fear the result of a hundred battles. If you know yourself but not the enemy, for every victory gained you will also suffer a defeat. If you know neither the enemy nor yourself, you will succumb in every battle." The same principle applies in the art of peace. Knowing China matters. It's important to note that to understand is not to agree, accept, acquiesce or appease. However, working with a genuine understanding of why China acts in certain ways means we stand a better chance of achieving the results we want to achieve.

How the West views China

Much of the discourse about China's changing role in the world expresses concern, if not alarm, about its growing influence. As Katherine Morton observes, "an underlying assumption … is that China is now moving inexorably in the direction of imperial expansion" and is "predominantly concerned with achieving hegemony in the South China Sea at any cost". An article in *The Atlantic* provides a representative example: "China has become a threat because its leaders are promoting a closed, authoritarian model as an alternative to democratic governance and free-market economics. The Chinese Communist Party is not only strengthening an internal system that stifles human freedom and extends its authoritarian control; it is also exporting that model and leading the development of new rules and a new international order that would make the world less free and less safe."

The highest political levels in the United States have made similar pronouncements. For example, in 2020, the State Department released a report which said: "The Chinese Communist Party (CCP) poses the central threat of our times, undermining the stability of the world to serve its own hegemonic ambitions." It sets out six ways the CCP is expanding its power and influence at the expense of others: predatory economic practices; military aggression in the Indo-Pacific region; the undermining of global norms and values; coercive tactics abroad; disregard for human rights; and environmental abuses.

Other analysts have argued that concerns around China's changing and growing role in the world are justified. For example,

Jessica Chen Weiss argues in a recent issue of *Foreign Affairs* that the concern over China in Washington (and plenty of other capitals, as she notes) has foundation: "Under President Xi Jinping especially, Beijing has grown more authoritarian at home and more coercive abroad. It has brutally repressed Uyghurs in Xinjiang, crushed democratic freedoms in Hong Kong, rapidly expanded its conventional and nuclear arsenals, aggressively intercepted foreign military aircraft in the East and South China Seas, condoned Russian President Vladimir Putin's invasion of Ukraine and amplified Russian disinformation, exported censorship and surveillance technology, denigrated democracies, worked to reshape international norms – the list could go on and will likely only get longer ..."

The attitude within China today is that it can never again allow itself to be weak

Australians tend to accept this view that China's changing role is a threat to the global order, and poses a potential risk to our national interests. We are particularly preoccupied with questions about how China behaves in the international system, because since May 2020 we have been the subject of a series of trade restrictions, including on exports to China of wine, barley, lobsters and coal. Very recently, high-level trade meetings have resumed and restrictions are being lifted – at least, they are said to have been lifted. These restrictions are generally understood as economic tools used by China for political coercion – to punish us for political misdemeanours.

The majority of English-language analysis of China in the international arena, as Rosemary Foot has observed, tends to follow one of two explanations of its behaviour: that its intentions are predominantly defensive – that is, China seeks a world safe for its own politics; or that they are offensive – meaning it aims to "diminish the space that is needed for liberal democracies to thrive". Either way, the dominant theme in the literature has a distinctly negative bent regarding China's role in shaping the global order.

This built-in negative bent affects how we interpret China's actions. Narratives around China's debt trap diplomacy – using unsustainable loans to gain economic, political and military influence – are a good example. Conventional wisdom tends to accept these interpretations of Chinese loans, and we can then make our own conclusions about what China wants to achieve and how we might deter or contain it. In Australia, the media has reported on claims that Pacific islands states such as Vanuatu and Tonga, as well as other nations in South-East Asia, are at risk of undue political influence from China because of unsustainable loans they have received.

However, over the past few years, research has either complicated the assumption that China is weaponising debt or contradicted it entirely. For years, academics such as Deborah Brautigam, Chris Alden, Erica S. Downs and Miwa Horono, among others, have been committed to myth-busting Chinese "truths" in English-language discourse. Indeed, as Miwa Hirono and Shogo Suzuki note, the "flurry of literature" on China as a threat to the interests of both Africa in particular and the international community more generally has created the necessity for a second genre of work whose primary purpose is myth-busting. Yet the myths continue to circulate unabashed.

How China views the world

What is missing from the current debate about China? I would argue that any analyst of China's behaviour on the world stage should not take even the smallest intellectual step without thinking about how China understands the "century of humiliation". Once again, this is not the same as accepting China's view of history as true, but to understand how China uses this constructed truth about itself and the world around it in its international relations. Described by some as China's "never again" mentality, the short version is that China was a historically peaceful and non-expansionist power and a dignified and well-respected global actor up until the Opium Wars of the mid-1800s. This was when "Western" actors deliberately attacked China to carve it up and bring it to its knees. This narrative is actively promoted in the post-1989 Patriotic Education curriculum, as well as in "red tourism", which constantly reminds visitors of China's greatness prior to Western aggression against it. The attitude within China today is that it can never again allow itself to be weak, backwards or vulnerable to external influences.

With the century of humiliation as a constant backdrop, the next step is to understand China's domestic goals, as these are what foreign policy exists to enable. According to experienced China observers, the core goal of the CCP, and therefore of the state administrative apparatus that is the government, is to reinforce the legitimacy and primacy of the Party and its governance system. This legitimacy depends on a well-understood and broadly accepted social contract that can be traced back roughly to 1989. In exchange for stability, security, increasing living standards and prosperity, and a realisation of China's national dignity, the Party expects non-interest and non-activity in politics from the Chinese people. This goal is reflected in the Party-state's articulation of its three key interests: protection of sovereignty and territorial integrity (Taiwan, Xinjiang, Tibet, the South China Sea), protection of its political model, and protection of its economic growth and development. These interests are, for China's leaders, fundamental and non-negotiable.

To achieve these core interests, the Chinese Party-state has released a slew of policy principles and goals. If we examine these, and the Chinese-language narratives around them, we can get a much better understanding of Beijing's domestic political and economic aims. President Xi Jinping's frameworks for becoming a "modern socialist nation" by 2035 include the New Development Concept, the Dual Circulation Strategy, Common Prosperity, and the 14th Five-Year Plan. These policies, which are based on a firm belief that the international environment is actively hostile towards China, aim to strengthen the CCP so it can confront and overcome what it sees as new and complex threats to China's interests.

Xi's policy framework reflects the preoccupations and pathologies of the narrative concerning the century of humiliation: the idea that China is situated in a hostile world that is full of Western-driven aggression determined to keep it down, but also that China is equally determined to throw off those shackles, to never be weak and vulnerable again, and to return to what it sees as its rightful place in the world, as a dignified, respected and peaceful global actor, not subject to "interference" in its "internal affairs", and with its sovereignty and territorial integrity accepted as sacrosanct.

In addition to the frameworks above, and just as firmly built on the century of humiliation narrative, are the Two Centenary Goals (or the Two Centenaries – *liangge yibai nian*). In 2017, President Xi announced these goals as a two-step plan "to build China into a great modern socialist country". The first step – building a moderately prosperous society in all respects (*xiaokang*) – was to be fulfilled by 2021, exactly 100 years after the founding of the Chinese Communist Party.

Fear of some kind of Western-backed "colour revolution" in China is very real

According to Chinese media, this ambition was achieved. As *The Global Times* proudly described it, the Chinese people took "more than two decades to throw off oppression as a semi-colonial, semi-feudal society and found the People's Republic of China in 1949. After the launch of reform and opening up in 1978, and through the continuous efforts of the Chinese people, China experienced the transformation from a huge, poor and backward country in the East into a thriving, socialist China" – notably, under and thanks to the leadership of the CCP.

The second goal, due by 2049, exactly 100 years after the establishment of the People's Republic of China, shifts China's development and progress focus to ask "what more China can do for itself and the world". This goal shows China's concerns about the world as a hostile and untrustworthy place – the century of humiliation narrative continued. *The Global Times*, which rarely strays far from the officially sanctioned position, notes that China, in this new century, faces "a more complicated international environment", when a "world in turbulence" is "experiencing profound changes not seen in a century".

To be more explicit, the challenge involves "intensifying tension between the two biggest world economies caused by Washington's hostility against China's peaceful development". Even more specifically, "the US and some of its Western followers who still dominate the current international system have already launched comprehensive suppression against China. This is the biggest risk and challenge from the outside world that we are facing right now," as Shen Yi, a professor at the School of International Relations and Public Affairs at the prestigious Fudan University, notes. For these reasons, it is now "time for China to actively guide the direction of the reform and improvement of globalisation", Wang Yiwei, director of the Institute of International Affairs at the also highly prestigious Renmin University of China, told the Chinese media outlet.

These policies provide clear sketch lines for how China sees itself in the world: as a country and a people labouring hard and working diligently to overthrow their past disadvantages and current challenges, largely caused by the West, which still today is trying to keep China from growing and developing. But at the same time, the "outside world" – and there's a big clue in that language about "us versus them" and "in versus out" – cannot be ignored. To develop, China has no option but to get more involved with a world that is turbulent and largely hostile to its interests. But it is hyper-anxious about unsavoury Western influences "seeping in at the seams" and undermining the CCP's legitimacy, as one of my interview respondents put it.

The language in English-language media such as *The Global Times* tends to be bold and confident, proud of China's achievements and ambitious about what the nation needs to and can achieve in the future. It is very much in line with what many describe as more muscular and assertive behaviour across China's trade and investment, military and diplomacy. However, messaging from China over the past few years has been inconsistent in tone. In 2020, Western media marvelled at the new "army" of "wolf warrior diplomats", who held nothing back when it came to telling it how it was (or how they thought it was, at least). But in 2021, according to the state-run news agency Xinhua, President Xi called for Chinese officials to tell a more positive story about itself, and create a more "credible, loveable and respectable China" – suggesting considerable concern at high levels that the world didn't really believe it, like it or think it worthy of respect.

These days, we see a bit of both approaches, and it can be confusing for outside analysts if we focus on that dual messaging as a means to understand China's view of the world. This mixed messaging reflects, within China, a fundamental contradiction, or *maodun*. This contradiction – between China's need for the outside world but its concomitant anxiety about it, between its nationalist pride and its need for "love" and respect – is founded on a deeper "identity dilemma", in which China's insecurities play a profound role in its approach to national security.

William Callahan has described China as a "pessoptimist nation". At the same time as Chinese identity proudly celebrates its ancient civilisation and past stature and achievements, it actively promotes the narrative of humiliation suffered at the hands of the West. Every step forward, every success, is lined with bitterness and resentment at how the West destroyed China and made this clawing-back necessary in the first place – and there is a visceral fear that the West is always and inevitably trying to do the same thing again. Policies and practices such as the ever-strengthening "Great Firewall", the new regulations on non-government organisations introduced in 2016, and the new anti-espionage law which took effect on 1 July 2023 clearly show how concerned the Chinese leadership is about Western ideas insidiously (or otherwise) infiltrating China's borders and threatening the CCP's legitimacy.

Fear of some kind of Western-backed "colour revolution" in China is very real.

How China views Australia

In Australia, we also want to know how China sees us. In what ways do we matter to China? Where does Australia fit into this worldview? The short answer is: peripherally.

Former Australian prime minister Kevin Rudd, now Australia's ambassador to the United States, describes China's view of the world in terms of concentric circles, which largely reflect geography – with the notable exception of the United States. Rudd describes how the countries that share physical borders with China matter the most, and how, in that schema, Australia matters very little.

This perspective is shared by many of the people I interviewed as part of this research. Australia matters for our resources – coal, iron ore and lithium – but is disparagingly understood as being the United States' "lapdog" or "deputy sheriff", and therefore is not to be entirely trusted; hence China's effort to diversify the sources of many of these commodities. While China needs Australian things right now, most of my interviewees agreed that if it came to the crunch, political concerns would override economic concerns. That is, the Chinese Party-state and people would be prepared to "eat bitterness" (*chi ku*) rather than be seen to roll over to foreigners.

Supporting the idea that Australia is relatively inconsequential to China are findings from research released in May by the University of Alberta. In *How China Sees the World in 2023*, Australia is reported as among the least influential nations in the world (along with Japan and India). While we're still seen as a favourable tourist destination, as

Wanning Sun notes in her analysis of the research, overall, "Australia doesn't rate very highly at all". Yet it is worth pointing out that, despite this ambivalence, or perhaps even because of it, the Chinese citizenry do not see "cultural and value differences as a significant barrier to collaboration".

Why does "why" matter?

As we have seen, there is a big difference between how "the West", in general, sees China and its growing role in the world and how China sees it. I do not intend to try to prove that one side is right or wrong. Rather, I want to ask how China's self-perception matters to the situation we find ourselves in.

Why bother asking "why"? What difference does it make if, as Katherine Morton argues, "China's ambition in the South China Sea is primarily driven by a historic mission to achieve its rightful status as a maritime nation, rather than by a grand design to achieve maritime hegemony"? Many China watchers and analysts argue that the only thing that matters is the result – that even if China is only trying to create a world that is safe for itself (the first of the two propositions Foot articulates), the outcome is still a concern.

In their paper on China as an illiberal hegemon, Darren Lim and G. John Ikenberry argue that while it might not be deliberate that China is exporting autocracy and undermining the liberal rules-based order, the way it goes about achieving its goals causes illiberalism to increase around the world. Examples include China's activities in the South

China Sea, its increasing influence in the United Nations, its "rogue" aid in exchange for political leverage, its building of overseas naval bases (or more accurately, naval base, singular – despite recent controversy about a Chinese naval base in Ream, Cambodia, currently the only one that exists in fact is the one opened in Djibouti in 2017), its provision of training for Solomon Islands police officers, and so on. These are all certainly complex issues that should not be ignored, and warrant our careful scrutiny. Whether or not China means to undermine the world order which we in the West think is fine the way it is, the argument goes, that is what it does. This prevailing view – that there is a problem with what China is doing – leads to the apparently self-evident next question: what should we do to stop it?

Quite simply, we may not be quite as right as we think we are

On the other hand, arguments suggesting we pause to undertake that necessary careful scrutiny and interrogate whether we actually know what it is we're responding to are harder to find. One example is Lyle Goldstein's thought-provoking 2015 book *Meeting China Halfway*. Goldstein argues that while it is not necessary to accept China's perspectives, it is imperative to understand them, in order to create the conditions necessary for meaningful cooperation between China and the United States and prevent a dangerous downward spiral in relations. Goldstein emphasises the different worldviews of the two actors: the US sees itself as a neutral mediator in the East, drawn by commercial opportunities; China sees the US as aggressive, imperialist and expansionist, and deliberately taking advantage of any sign of weakness to keep China down.

Another example is Alastair Iain Johnston's research from ten years back, "How New and Assertive Is China's New Assertiveness?", which asks just what the title suggests. Johnston concludes that despite the "rapidly spreading meme in US pundit and academic circles", only in the case of maritime disputes is there evidence for more assertive rhetoric and behaviour on China's part. In some purported examples of new assertiveness in US discourse, Johnston finds, China's policy had not changed; in others it was actually more moderate; and in still others it was "a predictable reaction to changed external conditions". Johnston demonstrates how the conventional wisdom around China's presumed growing assertiveness has three key analytical flaws. The first is that analysts have tended to emphasise the evidence that confirms their hypothesis of increasing Chinese assertiveness, creating the risk of exaggerating change and underestimating continuity (such as in US–China cooperation).

Another flaw is that analysts assume that what is happening now is new and different, not connected across time or comparable to different issues. An example is the coverage of Chinese diplomacy during the climate negotiations in Copenhagen in 2009, which was often described as newly assertive but was in fact a continuation of a bargaining position that had not changed much since 1990. As Johnston notes, what was new in Copenhagen was the Chinese delegation's lack of understanding of how much other countries had shifted their positions on climate change, and a growing willingness on the part of others to blame China as part of the problem. The delegation was not prepared for the degree of criticism it received.

A third flaw is that many analysts accept and promulgate the idea that China became newly assertive around 2010 as its leaders saw a shift in the distribution of global power. This, they argue, gave leaders an opportunity to change tack from former President Deng Xiaoping's long-held dictum to not hold the United States as an adversary. Johnston concludes, however, that the evidence for any such shift in perception shaping Chinese behaviour is thin at best.

These analyses show us that, quite simply, we may not be quite as right as we think we are. Our responses to China's growing role in the world too often overlook how the collective trauma (as China sees it) of its history of humiliation, victimisation and bullying – largely at the hands of the West – manifests as a passionate "never again" mentality. This readiness to accept and build on assumptions and conventional wisdom is not okay in a situation as critical as this one. We need to make sure we're as right as we can be in order to best respond. In a time of strategic rivalries and security dilemmas, making effective decisions requires the best possible information. If the conventional wisdom on which decision-makers rely is inaccurate by even a whisker, it risks increasing tensions and dramatic conflict, with unknowable consequences. As Morton notes, if we don't get this right, we may miss the ever-diminishing opportunity to achieve any kind of enduring power equilibrium.

In Australia's case, what might we gain by asking why? Why does Australia's focus on certain values matter so much to China? Why do the Chinese become so outraged when we do what we think is right and call them out on what we see as transgressions? For example, why did they respond – and are we even correct in characterising it as a response? – to Australia's call for an inquiry into the origins of COVID-19 with trade restrictions and denial of high-level relations? The general belief is that China has used its weight to punish us and coerce us, often economically, into doing what it wants. There is a growing industry in Australia examining China's geo-economic statecraft, including at the Australian National University and the Lowy Institute. But are we correct? Why does China think that taking this kind of approach will succeed? What does "success" look like to China? Why did they seem to change their mind about the trade restrictions on Australian goods such as barley and wine earlier this year? Did they get what they wanted or did Australia cleverly outplay them? What does Beijing, in fact, "want"?

The truth is, we haven't got good answers to these questions. Rather than taking the time to interrogate our assumptions and dig deeply into complexity, we tend to rely on intellectual short cuts. We bandy about over-simple understandings and glibly reiterated assumptions that, over time, become accepted as truths – like the idea that China "obviously" wants to expand its power and influence, and to be the regional, if not global, hegemon. These "truths", in turn, become the departure platform for the next set of assumptions, which themselves become truths, and so on. We rarely stop to ask: given that power is a means to an end rather than an end in itself, what does it mean to China? How would China use its increased power and influence?

Take, for example, the idea that "deterrence" is a useful means of moderating and constraining China's "increasingly assertive", "provocative" or "belligerent" behaviour.

Are we confident that China, with all its particular self-perceptions and worldviews, will interpret our deterrence measures in such a way that it is effectively deterred? Or might it be further provoked, given its view of itself and its position in the world?

Our current knowledge base … is not fit for purpose in such complex and nuanced circumstances

Have we critically examined our efforts at deterrence so far? The Taiwan Strait crisis of 1995–1996 is often used as an example of successful US deterrence against Chinese aggression. These events were very complex, but at their simplest: in 1995 Taiwan's president was granted a visa to visit the United States, and did so. Beijing then undertook a series of military exercises and military tests in and around the Taiwan Strait, which were meant to signal displeasure at the visit, to intimidate Taiwan in the lead-up to its next presidential election and, more broadly, to send a strong signal to Taiwan that anything even remotely conceivable as nose-thumbing at the PRC, let alone pursuing independence, was absolutely unacceptable. In response, US President Bill Clinton (incidentally, in an election year) ordered several naval vessels to the Taiwan Strait, in what has been described as the biggest display of US military power in Asia since the Vietnam War.

Can we say, as the conventional wisdom holds, that these US demonstrations of substantial force and strength were effective deterrents? The United States' objective was to deter prospective Chinese aggression against Taiwan. No aggression occurred at that time. Is there a direct causal link? How did those moves affect the broader relationship and China's views towards Taiwan and the United States? Did US countermeasures solve that problem once and for all? Or, as Douglas Porch from the US Naval War College argues, is there in fact very little evidence to support the thesis that US actions effectively deterred Beijing aggression towards Taiwan in either the short or the longer term? Did those actions perhaps actually incentivise the PRC to harden its resolve and develop new generations of weapons that will make it far more difficult for the United States to counter any PRC pressure on Taiwan in the future? Did they kick the proverbial can down the road, creating an even more intractable problem, one even more difficult to peacefully resolve?

These are open questions. The point is that they need to be asked much more than they are. Our current knowledge base – from which we design the means to effectively achieve whatever it is we want to achieve in our relationship with China – is not fit for purpose in such complex and nuanced circumstances. We really have very little idea if China will act, when it will act, or how it will act in the future.

So where are we?

How, then, does China understand that it needs to achieve its domestic goals of modernisation and development? Through engaging with the "outside world". What does China see as the biggest threats to its interests? The outside world. Herein lies China's great conundrum. It needs the world to achieve its domestic imperatives, but it fundamentally mistrusts the world. However, Western approaches to China tend to neglect these perceptions, considering them inaccurate and irrelevant.

The language we see is about China's rise as a major power, China's growing influence, how China uses its increasing economic and political power to assert its influence, China as a risk to the rules-based order, China's desire to be a regional and/or global hegemon, and so on. These descriptions are ubiquitous. Writers and analysts use these phrases in the way that once reminded George Orwell of building "prefabricated hen-houses". That is to say, they are often accepted and used without critique or interrogation as the intellectual basis on which further conclusions are then built. It's simply accepted as true that this is who and what China is (autocrat, et cetera), and that this is what China is trying to achieve (influence, hegemony, et cetera). Rather than selecting words about China carefully, for the sake of their actual meaning, we use and accept pre-assembled and mass-produced phrases. The ideas behind them are no longer deemed worthy of interrogation – they have become the "conventional wisdom".

Relying on uninterrogated conventional wisdom is simply not sufficient in these volatile circumstances. As Orwell famously argued, language is not neutral – it is highly political. It creates truths. Similarly, Johnston notes that how adversaries are described reverberates in domestic politics, narrowing public discourse and habituating conventional wisdom, which ultimately makes it more difficult for other voices to challenge policy orthodoxies and narrows the range of options available to decision-makers. If we are not correct in our understandings of China's motivations, then the strategies and solutions we come up with will be inappropriate, ineffective and possibly counterproductive. The diagnosis affects the prognosis as well as the treatment. If we are wrong, even slightly, in our fundamental assumptions, we are bound to find ourselves in a negative spiral from which it is harder and harder to pull ourselves out.

In a situation as critical as the geopolitical one we face with China, if our language is politically loaded and our assumptions are questionable, then we need to review and critique them. Doing so might slow us on our trajectory, which is, if not hurtling, then certainly bumping along at a rollicking pace towards increased tensions and conflict. It is surely worth allowing ourselves to consider a different approach, to achieve different and, perhaps, more positive outcomes. If in the art of war it is essential to know your enemy, then surely, in the pursuit of peace, it is even more important to know exactly who and what you are dealing with. ■

NO DAYLIGHT

Inside Labor's decision to back AUKUS

Margaret Simons

Tell the story baldly, and it is beyond belief. Over thirty-six hours in September 2021, not only did the Australian government announce a big change of tack on Australian defence policy, betraying the trust of one ally and further enmeshing the nation with the United States and Britain, but the alternative government backed the move after just a two-hour briefing.

AUKUS, the trilateral security pact with the United States and the United Kingdom under which Australia will become one of only seven countries with nuclear-powered submarines, became bipartisan policy literally overnight. Or that is what the messy first draft of history – the media's reporting of these events – suggests.

The truth is more complex, nuanced, contingent and contextual. There is a prehistory to AUKUS and how, despite many questions and concerns which have been only partly addressed in the public conversation, it gained the backing of two Australian governments.

In this prehistory, the submarines are not the only, and not the most consequential element. The driving force is a recognition that the United States has lost its technological primacy over China – that it is no longer clear that it can win either a hot or a cold war. In short, the US needs its allies. Donald Trump talked about them having to pay their way. The Biden administration's language is less transactional, but the message is the same. They are expected to step up.

Meanwhile, in Australia, there has been a slow building of consensus, the origins of which go back almost twenty years and are embedded within the security establishment in all three AUKUS nations. Depending on your point of view, this has led the Labor left to sell out on its historical opposition to all things nuclear and its advocacy of a more independent foreign policy. Or, to take another view – the view of Labor's parliamentary leadership team – it has made a necessary adjustment to a changed world, in which many superficially contradictory things are true at once. In this worldview, independence, national sovereignty and even peace can only be safeguarded by a tighter, more militarised alliance.

Prime Minister Scott Morrison, whose government had been cooking the AUKUS deal in secret for almost two years, briefed the Labor leadership team on 14 September 2021, ahead of the public announcement on 15 September.

Later that day, there was an emergency Shadow Cabinet meeting. AUKUS was the only topic of discussion. Questions were asked, and the discussion was lengthy and contentious, sources say. But the prevailing mood was awareness that an election was less than nine months away and Labor was on track to win.

"A clear decision had been made … that Labor could win the election if it made Scott Morrison the key issue. But it could not allow itself to be drawn or diverted into any other side journey … we could not give Scott Morrison anything he could use." Key to this was the memory of the 2019 election and how a scare campaign about Labor's tax and spending policies had led to an unexpected defeat. And so Shadow Cabinet ticked off on AUKUS.

The next day, news of the AUKUS agreement had leaked to the media. That meant members of the Labor caucus had about two hours in which to prepare questions for the leadership team, before they were called together.

Caucus was not asked to endorse the decision of Shadow Cabinet. It was merely being informed

Kim Carr, the longest-serving member of the Australian Senate and a former minister and shadow minister, spoke first, followed by about eight others. He recalls that the concerns raised were "entirely predictable" and included the cost, whether the subs would lead to nuclear proliferation and whether Australia would retain control over how they were used. Carr rubbished the idea that the submarines could be operated without a domestic nuclear industry, even though Albanese had ruled that out as a condition of Labor's support.

But caucus was not asked to endorse the decision of Shadow Cabinet. It was merely being informed.

The Morrison government had successfully kept the development of the AUKUS agreement confidential. Even close observers had no hint of what was coming, although news of increasing concerns about the French submarine contract was circulating. But some people on both sides of politics were less surprised than others.

Ross Babbage is the CEO of the Strategic Forum think tank, whose goal is to foster "thought on Australia's security challenges", including through hosting off-the-record and closed workshops, "generally in partnership with relevant senior officials", according to the organisation's website. Babbage has been a regular in the corridors of Parliament House and ministerial offices for many years.

In late 2011 and in May 2012 – four years before the Turnbull government negotiated the agreement with the French to build twelve conventionally powered submarines – Babbage wrote a couple of extraordinarily prescient articles for *The Diplomat*. He argued that the best submarines for Australia would be nuclear-powered Virginia-class boats, leased or bought second-hand. "It would be sensible to have discussions with both the U.S. and U.K. governments," he wrote. And, if Virginia-class boats were chosen, they would operate "in very close cooperation with U.S. boats in Pacific and Indian Ocean waters. There are likely to be substantial advantages flowing to both countries from joint basing, logistic support, training and many other aspects."

In his second piece, Babbage said "this would herald a new level of operational partnership with the United States and substantially strengthen Australia's contribution to allied operations in the Western Pacific. Canberra's diplomatic clout in Washington and across the Asia-Pacific would be greatly enhanced."

Interviewed for this article, Babbage says he had no advance notice of the AUKUS announcement – the secret was indeed tightly held. But nor did it entirely surprise him, because since he'd written those articles, he had been talking to the Americans informally and knew that they were open to the possibility of sharing nuclear submarine technology with Australia.

Babbage says that eight years ago he made "informal inquiries" of people in the United States about selling or leasing nuclear-powered submarines to Australia, and he got three waves of response over about twelve months, with the last from a source in the White House. The message was: "If you really want to be serious let's sit down and negotiate the best arrangement. But in principle, we're prepared to contemplate it."

In Babbage's view, a decade ago many in Labor were instinctively against the idea of nuclear-powered submarines. Those who were open to the idea didn't think it was urgent or necessary to have what would inevitably be a contentious debate within the party. But, he says, that has changed in the last five years, due in part to "a series of members of the parliamentary Labor Party who've had classified briefings, and a broader range of people who've actually done some homework on the deteriorating security situation in East Asia ... And they realised pretty quickly that the circumstances we now face have changed and are continuing to change quite rapidly." They concluded, he says, that conventional submarines were unlikely to meet the challenge of the next few decades.

So why has AUKUS had such strenuous pushback from former Labor government ministers, most notably Paul Keating? And what is it that changed the view of their successors in the Labor leadership?

The deteriorating security situation, Babbage says, has led to "a huge gulf" between those who closely follow the intelligence and the dialogue in the security establishment – "those who put in the work", as he puts it – and those who don't. The public conversation and awareness lags far behind, he says. His think tank follows everything President Xi Jinping says publicly, he claims, accessing translated speeches and policy announcements and analysing them promptly. Meanwhile, the Australian media reports voluminously on every move by Biden and Trump, but fails to report important speeches and statements by Xi and his colleagues. "The country is ill-served," he concludes.

And what is it in the intelligence that justifies a change of view?

Babbage is guarded, but talks about China's changing circumstances and its more assertive international behaviour – its economic problems and its shrinking population, together with "what they're saying daily about things like Taiwan". There is also the "nearly one million people that they have employed in planning and undertaking political coercion, interference in foreign governments, manipulation of social media and subversion".

How is AUKUS relevant to this, given that the first submarines, optimistically, won't be available for decades?

That question brings us to what is generally described as the second pillar of AUKUS – the part that is about "advanced capability sharing" between the three partners. The AUKUS announcement specified quantum computing, cyberwarfare, artificial intelligence and undersea hypersonics. This pillar, according to a range of commentators, is more important than the submarines. The submarines won't be in the water for decades. But the technological sharing is expected to be making a difference within the next three to five years.

Allan Behm, now the director of the international and security affairs program at the progressive Australia Institute think tank, is a former senior adviser to Foreign Minister Penny Wong, when she was shadow minister. He too was taken by surprise by AUKUS, and concerned that Labor leapt on board so quickly.

He recalls: "In the few days after, I made sure that the Opposition frontbench heard an alternative view, which was 'Hey, look, we didn't really need to do that. We needed to say, that's a really interesting, constructive idea. We'll have a very close look at it when we win government and if we find merit in it, then we will prosecute it.' And it's fair to say that a number of them had already thought about that approach. But there was, I think, very deep fear about being in the slightest bit wedged on this."

Other close observers within Labor had a less optimistic, and perhaps more realistic, view.

Gareth Evans, who was foreign minister during the Hawke/Keating governments, believes that if Labor had been "the least bit equivocal" about AUKUS, the 2022 election would have been fought on national security, with the Coalition government depicting Labor as scuppering AUKUS, undermining the alliance and eroding the United States' commitment to the region. This might well have been true, given that the US had made clear to Morrison that AUKUS must be bipartisan if it was to work. The government had assured the Americans that Labor would come on board – a prediction that proved correct.

Evans understood the "desperate, desperate desire not to be wedged", but he also judged that there was enough justification for AUKUS "to hang your hat on intellectually". Nuclear propulsion was clearly superior. He did not regard subs with closed nuclear power units as a breach of nuclear proliferation obligations and thought the left of the party should "have a Bex and get on with the business of winning an election". He had questions about "the fit-for-purpose issue and the sovereignty issue" but thought that once Labor won power, there would be plenty of time for review, negotiation and readjustment.

His doubts have grown since Albanese, Biden and British prime minister Rishi Sunak announced the detail in March 2023, including an estimated $368 billion cost over three decades, and a plan to buy at least three second-hand Virginia-class submarines – as Babbage anticipated all those years before – ahead of the AUKUS-manufactured boats.

"The cost has been explained, and it is gigantic," Evans says. "The enmeshment with the USA has been explained, and is more extensive than I appreciated in September 2021. It involves not only more interoperability but more co-dependence with the USA." That worries him.

But what has not been explained, Evans says, is "the degree of military benefit ... how three boats on station at any given time are going to be better able to perform necessary military tasks than cheaper conventional submarines." And if the idea is to make sure that the US remains engaged in the region and will be there if we need its help, "it seems to me that we're sacrificing a huge amount of sovereign agency for a return that we're utterly unable to be confident about".

Evans is not alone in his view. Allan Gyngell, who has been described by Penny Wong as one of Australia's leading foreign and strategic policy thinkers, said in a podcast shortly before his death in May 2023 that he was "persuadable" about AUKUS but had not been persuaded. There had been no public conversation, no sufficient explanation. Gyngell went on to remark that he would not have to rename any new editions of his classic history of foreign policy, *Fear of Abandonment*.

Evans remarks that Australian strategic policy is now caught between that fear and another: fear of entrapment, of Australia being entirely tied to US strategic policy, powerless to make its own decisions.

So how, given all the questions about AUKUS, was Labor persuaded?

Babbage says that among those in Labor who have "done the work" and been receptive to briefings are some who "fly beneath the radar, but are influential". He names Peter Khalil, the member for Wills, who entered parliament in 2016.

Before his election, Khalil worked for the Department of Defence and for the Department of Foreign Affairs and Trade, and he was a national security adviser to Prime Minister Kevin Rudd. Crucially, he has served on, and is the current chair of, the Parliamentary Joint Committee on Intelligence and Security, which oversees the intelligence agencies.

Khalil was also taken by surprise by AUKUS, but says he understood it "immediately". "I was like, 'Okay, that makes sense.' I understand what they've been doing. They've been discussing it between the three countries and it's a big deal."

On that high-pressure day in September 2021, Khalil had several conversations with the Labor leadership group, and articulated his views and advice. He was in favour of backing AUKUS. It answered concerns he had for a long time about the appropriateness of the French conventionally powered subs. More than that, he understood the significance of the wider agreement to share technology. "I saw AUKUS for what it was, which is a trilateral technology agreement, if you like, a capability agreement."

Khalil talks about the briefings he has had over many years, and his own knowledge of "what I know has become a cliché" – the most dangerous security environment in our lifetime. Asked for detail, he says: "The level of political interference in our political system, the level of espionage, the level of sabotage … are just through the roof. And most people don't see that because it's not made public. And this is the challenge of having a public discussion. How much do you talk about this without scaring people? And you can't talk about it too much because of what is underway to try and prevent those attacks."

Asked the question posed by Gareth Evans – how would nuclear submarines answer the threats, particularly since only a few would be in service at any one time? – Khalil says the same criticisms could be made of the Collins-class submarines. The key difference is detectability.

As to what the subs will do – he says not everything can be talked about, but it is not only about defence but also intelligence. "Making sure that we have a very clear picture of what is happening across the region in the space that is the most critical for us … And the job that they will do, without going into great detail,

The standard line coming out of Canberra is that AUKUS will simply be "too big to fail"

is more than just protecting the shipping lanes. There is an intelligence element to these operations … making sure there's a real understanding of the environment and who's doing what in that environment." Thanks to their lack of detectability, the AUKUS submarines will simply do the job better.

But with the subs being decades away, Khalil agrees that it is the second pillar – the sharing of advanced capacities – that will have the biggest impact in both the short and long terms.

In the prehistory of AUKUS, one name comes up repeatedly: Andrew Shearer, who since his appointment by the Morrison government has been the director-general of the Office of National Intelligence. He is often referred to in the media as "Australia's top spy". As well as holding senior posts advising Abbott and Morrison, he has been a senior adviser on Asia-Pacific security at the Center for Strategic and International Studies in Washington DC – a think tank that has close relations with the Pentagon and US security agencies. In 2019 he was appointed as cabinet secretary to Morrison, and then moved to the ONI job at the end of 2020.

It was Shearer who, in April 2021, met with Joe Biden's top Indo-Pacific adviser, Kurt Campbell, in a discussion that has been reported to be the AUKUS "clincher". It is "that bastard Shearer" whom, sources say, the French most blame for their contract to build submarines being scuppered. It was Shearer who, before that contract was signed, as national security adviser to Prime Minister Tony Abbott, reportedly wanted to have Japan, not France, build the submarines.

Former PM Turnbull – who is still arguing that the French could have met our submarine needs – remembers Shearer as being "very, very, very close" to the US establishment. Other gossip from Canberra has Shearer allegedly "going rogue" under Morrison, having meetings with a wide array of US and UK intelligence people, often with nobody else present and no formal notes being taken. He was at the forefront of AUKUS – a linchpin.

When Shearer was appointed to the ONI job, a strategically placed news story quoted senior Labor sources as saying he was too partisan for the job. Labor had told Morrison that it did not have confidence in him. But since then, Labor has changed its tune. In a profile written by *The Australian*'s Greg Sheridan in December 2021, Albanese said of Shearer: "He is always courteous and available and presents intelligent and factual material in a clear and concise manner. It has been good to develop such a positive relationship with him." And when Albanese jetted off to Japan the day after being elected, Shearer was with him.

Insider gossip suggests that Shearer is no longer quite as influential as he was under Morrison – that he sits further down the table, rather than at the right hand of the prime minister. His position as the head of ONI is a five-year statutory appointment, which has another two years to run. There is no sign he will be removed before that.

Meanwhile, Khalil indicates he has confidence in all the heads of Australia's security agencies. He declines to comment on any individual, and emphasises that he is making a general point when he says: "If security and intelligence heads are doing their jobs, serving the government and providing intelligence assessments to the Prime Minister and Cabinet in a non-partisan way, it doesn't matter who they worked for in the past, in my view. You become partisan if you do your job in a partisan way, and if they are doing their jobs properly, then they are not partisan."

The media team at ONI was asked if it would be possible to speak to Shearer to inform this article. After a month of silence, it replied: "We are unable to assist with your enquiry on this occasion."

But the ideas and connections that guide Shearer, and that have in turn convinced both sides of politics about AUKUS, can be divined from his public appearances, and in particular a panel discussion he chaired, hosted by the Australian Strategic Policy Institute, in April 2023.

Shearer had assembled an impressive panel. It included Sir Stephen Lovegrove, the UK national security adviser and former secretary of the

Ministry of Defence. Lovegrove, Shearer told the audience, was "one of the architects of AUKUS" and the "linchpin" of the UK's involvement. Also on the panel was Sue Gordon, the United States' former principal deputy director of national intelligence, described by Shearer as "a great partner of Australia over many years". The panel was rounded out by Michelle Simmons, Australia's leading quantum scientist and the founder of the first Australian quantum computing company.

The focus of the panel was "AUKUS, Technology and the Role of Intelligence". Before he had even introduced his panellists, Shearer gave an extraordinarily frank spiel. It was not about American strength. It was about weakness. "We're seeing our longstanding technological edge starting to erode. In some cases, that edge is totally gone," he said.

The panellists picked up on that theme. Lovegrove spoke almost disparagingly about the focus on submarines. "AUKUS in the newspapers is typically accompanied by pictures of absolutely gigantic bits of ocean-going kit," he said, but just as important, perhaps more important, was the sharing of technology among liberal democracies. Lovegrove described how authoritarian regimes could harness capabilities across private and public entities. Liberal democracies relied more on the free market, and that could be a weakness. Mechanisms had to be found to pull together expertise across allied countries, and across industry and academia.

Gordon picked up the theme with an almost religious fervour. AUKUS, she said, was part of giving "free and open societies" a new "quest" and a "bold mission". When it came to capability sharing: "We're still dragging the Cold War with us … if we don't set a new quest …

something that you must do, you can be really bogged down … I know that the strength of the West … of free and open societies, is that we have friends, and we are able to bring that to bear in times of crisis and conflict to great global societal advantage."

Challenging the idea that AUKUS was about the "Anglosphere", the panel talked about plans to include other countries of the region in the second pillar of AUKUS. Japan and Korea were mentioned.

From there, they moved to a discussion – opaque to the non-cognoscenti – about data encryption and quantum computing. Members of the Australian intelligence community are reluctant to spell out what is meant by these coded discussions, but information freely available in the United States sheds some light. The prediction is that quantum computing – a rapidly emerging technology that harnesses the laws of quantum mechanics to solve problems too complex for classical computers – will soon mean that encrypting data will be pointless.

China is ahead in quantum computing. The consultancy Booz Allen Hamilton has suggested it is already gathering encrypted data on individuals, government and defence secrets and more, with an eye to the day, coming very soon, when it will be able to be decrypted.

Meanwhile, the FBI says on its website that counterintelligence and economic espionage are the "top counterintelligence priority" for the agency. China's aim, the FBI says, is to control entire supply chains. And in this the Indo-Pacific is key.

Other elements of AUKUS pillar two include underwater drones that might be able to detect and block attacks, augmenting submarines – both our current fleet and the AUKUS boats, if and when they arrive. Other technologies are aimed at blocking cyberattacks. Home Affairs minister Clare O'Neil said recently that attacks on Optus, Medibank and Latitude Financial were the tip of the iceberg and the government was preparing for more breaches attempting to cripple critical infrastructure assets such as water supply and the electricity grid.

These, on top of submarines, are the arguments that have convinced Australian leaders on both sides of politics. This is a large part of why AUKUS is bipartisan. The leadership of our political parties believe that what is required to defend Australia has changed.

The United States has been struggling to assert its role in the Indo-Pacific for decades, and failing to do so. Ashley Townshend, senior fellow for Indo-Pacific security at the Carnegie Endowment for International Peace, traces this back to George W. Bush, who wanted to found a "federated network of allies" to check China's rise. That was overtaken by the September 11 terrorist attacks and the "War on Terror". President Obama talked about a pivot to the Pacific but failed to follow through. The legacy of failure means, Townshend has written, that the US can no longer guarantee a favourable regional balance of power by itself. Hence the Biden administration's emphasis on strengthening the military capacities of allies and partners. AUKUS is "the most consequential example of this agenda".

But Townshend has also cast doubt on whether the United States is capable of fulfilling the commitments implied by AUKUS when it comes to information and technology sharing. In a podcast put out by the ANU National Security College, Townshend said that the three AUKUS partners have different ideas about what pillar two of AUKUS is about. Australia wants access to long-range strike capabilities and underwater technology, and to benefit from US expertise and technology. The United Kingdom is more concerned with industrial policy – finding things it can sell to the Australians and the Americans. As for the US, it wants to "hoover up" the niche capabilities and competencies that Australia and the UK have on offer, to its own advantage.

Meanwhile, Townshend said, the current export control regime in the United States was antiquated and instinctively secretive. "It is not fit for purpose in an era of strategic competition, and it is certainly ill equipped to implement the vision that is infused within AUKUS," he said. He queried whether the "political momentum" behind AUKUS is "high enough to drive the kind of bureaucratic reforms needed".

As for the reservations about whether the allies can really carry it off, about the possible failures of will and capacity in the United States and the United Kingdom, the standard line coming out of Canberra is that AUKUS will simply be "too big to fail".

Foreign Minister Penny Wong rose to her feet to address the National Press Club on 17 April 2023, a month after she had been excoriated by Paul Keating in the same forum. Reporting her speech, the media framed it as her response to Keating. That meant they missed the rest of what she said. That was a shame, because it was a significant speech – a contribution to that all-important public conversation.

And, in her words, the differences between the United States' and Australia's priorities were apparent. Wong delineated a subtle foreign policy, one in which the US is Australia's indispensable ally – but not one in which Australia is necessarily in lockstep with the superpower's attempts to remain dominant in our region.

It is likely that nobody has gone into the Oval Office at the White House and told Joe Biden – or Trump, or Obama, or George W. Bush – that the United States has to accept that it is no longer Top Nation. That it has to make room for China's rise. That its role was merely to provide "balance". But that message could be read from what Wong said.

Taking as her topic how to "avert war and maintain peace – and more than that, how we shape a region that reflects our national interests", she eschewed, as she has in many speeches before, thinking only in terms of great-power primacy. "Many commentators and strategists ... love a binary," she observed. "And the appeal of a binary is obvious. Simple, clear choices. Black and white."

In an implicit hit at both Keating and the commentator Hugh White, who has suggested that China has already won the strategic competition and Australia should learn to live with it, Wong said: "Australia's foreign policy, at its best, has never simply been 'what you do with the great powers' ... There have been those throughout Australia's history who have thought our foreign policy should simply be to attach ourselves to a great power. Now some imply we should attach ourselves to what they anticipate will be a hegemonic China. But ... we will always pursue greater self-reliance and a more active foreign policy."

And that was all about the agency of middle powers. A "funda-mental principle", Wong said, was to build partnerships with a view to shaping the region, including the behaviour of superpowers. AUKUS made Australia a better, stronger partner to other middle powers.

China would continue to be Australia's largest trading partner. China would continue to use "every tool at its disposal to maximise its own resilience and influence ... Yet we need not waste energy with shock or outrage at China seeking to maximise its advantage. Instead, we channel our energy in pressing for our own advantage."

America remained "the indispensable power ... but the nature of that indispensability has changed," she said. "America is central to balancing a multipolar region. Many who take self-satisfied potshots at Ameri-ca's imperfections would find the world a lot less satisfactory if America ceased to play its role." But "we cannot just leave it to the US. All countries of the region must exercise their agency through diplomatic, economic and other engagement to maintain the region's balance – and to uphold the norms and rules that have underpinned decades of peace and pros-perity. And this balance must be underwritten by military capability."

And that was what AUKUS was all about.

This is the message that Australia has been selling throughout the region. And, insiders are quick to point out, despite reservations expressed by Indonesia and Malaysia, the response to AUKUS within ASEAN has been largely muted, with notes of support.

Peter Khalil, whose electorate covers some of the most left-wing suburbs in Australia, has faced a motion against AUKUS in one of his branches, with former Hawke government minister Brian Howe sitting in the front row. Khalil attended and argued the case. He expects to have to do a lot more of that. Keating, he says, did a public service in promoting a debate about defence policy, even though he doesn't agree with his conclusions. Australia no longer has the luxury of not thinking or knowing about the risks we face. We can no longer leave it all to the US.

These, then, are the arguments and conversations that have convinced Labor. It is not only about American strength but also about its weakness, even as it remains "indispensable". At first, it seemed that the consensus in the parliamentary leadership team would not hold for the party as a whole. State Labor conferences saw strong opposition. But at the national conference in August, the party confirmed a profound and consequential policy shift.

In a stage-managed debate that followed weeks of behind-the-scenes manoeuvres, Marles and the defence industry minister, Pat Conroy, moved a 32-paragraph statement arguing the case for AUKUS as crucial for national security, and making assurances that Labor will "ensure that all Australian warships, including submarines, are Australian sovereign assets, commanded by Australian officers and under the sovereign control of the Australian Government". There were heckles from the rank-and-file members, but also claps when Conroy declared that "strength deters war, appeasement invites conflict".

Albanese argued there was "no security in isolation". He said Australia was a mature nation that "understands that a bright future calls for more than sunny optimism … We have to analyse the world as it is rather than as we would want it to be. We have to bring our defence capabilities up to speed and AUKUS is central to that."

He got a standing ovation from about four-fifths of the conference, and the Marles and Conroy statement was carried on the voices. Those opposed to AUKUS were clearly outnumbered. But what if both governments – Labor and the Coalition – got it wrong?

James Curran, professor of modern history at Sydney University, has recently released *Australia's China Odyssey*, which charts how Australian attitudes to China have oscillated between threat and opportunity. He worries that the "threat narrative" has now become dogma. In an interview for this piece, Curran said: "The threat assessments from the security agencies get more and more alarmist, but where is the evidence? Where is the evidence that China has successfully interfered in the legislative arena of Australian politics – whether any move by any parliament in the country had been materially affected? I mean, have they actually changed or influenced the making of any laws?"

He told an audience at the Sydney Writers' Festival in May 2023 that despite calming the rhetoric, the Labor government had "broadly accepted the strategic judgements and assessments of its predecessor when it comes to … China". As a result, he said, the degree of enmeshment with United States represented by AUKUS now made it "impossible for Canberra to say no to Washington in the event of a war with China". And, he warned, there are members of the Republican Party in the United States who are urging a policy of Taiwan declaring independence.

That would be the equivalent of shouting, "Bring it on!"

*

Is AUKUS really too big to fail? Common sense suggests that over the thirty years of the agreement, a lot will change. Including governments. Some scientists predict that by 2050 technology will have rendered the oceans transparent, making submarines redundant. There are questions about both political will and industrial capacity in each of the three partner countries.

Surely, I said to a government source, there must be a plan B, if not plans C and D? Of course, I was told. There was constant work underway, many contingency plans, even if the public statements were universally positive rhetoric.

"If not AUKUS," Khalil asks, "then what?" The only answer he has heard Keating spell out is more conventional submarines – which means sacrificing better capacity for no good reason.

Meanwhile, Allan Behm reflects that the world of international relations is essentially chaotic. "And the most interesting thing in it is human agency. And because human beings are so bloody strange, it's no wonder that we've got things that are floating around both true and untrue all at the same time." Foreign policy is not like applied mechanics, where all you need is a manual. "We never have the total truth about anything," he says. In the end, it will be human choices that determine the way forward.

And so AUKUS, artefact of the new "quest" or "grand project", lands like a stone in an already troubled pond. ■

USUAL SUSPECTS

Our China-obsessed approach to foreign interference is self-defeating

Yun Jiang

Consider this: I was born in the People's Republic of China; I was a member of the Chinese Communist Party's Young Pioneers and used to regularly salute the party flag; half my family are members of the CCP; and my grandfather was a senior officer in the People's Liberation Army. How do these facts shape your perceptions of me? Would you think that I am an agent of the PRC? Would you call up the national security hotline and make a report about me when you see me sitting in a cafe outside a government agency in Canberra?

In fact, my background is far from unique. The CCP is an inextricable part of growing up for virtually everyone in the PRC. Many of the most talented, intelligent and ambitious people in that country have joined the Party. And most families would have been touched by war and have a relative who served in the military.

Back in 2020, some Australian senators certainly thought my ethnic background was suspicious. They asked a group of Chinese Australians appearing at a Senate inquiry, including me, to prove our loyalty to Australia by denouncing the CCP – a request not made to any other Australian appearing at the inquiry. The price of admission to the Senate, it seemed, was to thump our chests, declare the CCP were the baddies and draw a line in the sand marking ourselves out as the goodies. That unfortunate episode came amid heightened concerns about espionage and foreign interference by the PRC.

These concerns have not gone away. In his 2023 threat assessment, Mike Burgess, the head of the Australian Security Intelligence Organisation, said, "Australia is facing an unprecedented challenge from espionage and foreign interference." This is not new – it has been described as "unprecedented" for more than five years, ever since Burgess's predecessor, Duncan Lewis, used the term in 2017. Burgess also called on those who believe foreign interference is no big deal and can be safely managed to "reflect on their commitment to Australia's democracy, sovereignty and values".

These comments reflect the view of one particular agency within the bureaucracy – and we might note that that agency's understanding of "democracy" and "values" has in the past led to surveillance of Indigenous activists and anti-war protestors. The public should therefore listen with a sceptical ear, even though it does not have access to ASIO's classified information.

In this essay, I take up Burgess's challenge and reflect on how the public discourse on foreign influence and interference in Australia has affected its democracy, sovereignty and values.

Certainly, there are legitimate concerns about foreign interference. Broadly, Australia faces two types of risk stemming from the PRC's influence and interference activities. The first, which has been the focus of the Australian government, is the national security risk. This centres on policy and electoral influence and interference, such as lobbying and spreading of disinformation.

Freedom of speech requires that PRC citizens should be able to advocate for their political views peacefully

The second, which tends to be the focus of human rights organisations, is the civil liberty risk. This centres on concerns that PRC activities threaten freedom of speech, including the suppression of dissent and censorship outside its borders. The target of this sort of influence is generally people in the Chinese diaspora, including international students from the PRC.

However, the singular focus on the PRC as the source of interference has been counterproductive, and threatens to damage the very democracy the anti-interference measures are designed to protect. This focus on the PRC has been particularly damaging for Chinese Australians.

Chinese Australians are under tremendous pressure to self-censor. Some are wary of expressing views aligned with the PRC, for fear of being labelled agents of interference and having their reputation ruined. Others are wary of publicly criticising the PRC, for fear that it might damage their prospects of obtaining a visa or endanger their relatives in China.

Yet over the last five years, many in the national security community seem to have accepted these burdens placed on Chinese Australians as "collateral damage" – unfortunate and unintended, but necessary to ensure Australia is free from the PRC's influence.

Instead of targeting a single country, the government should aim to combat the various tools that are used by foreign countries – including the PRC – to conduct interference. Such an approach will reduce collateral damage, will better target interference activities and, simultaneously, will strengthen Australia's democracy.

Foreign interference and foreign influence

Influence and interference, although often treated as interchangeable, are distinct concepts. Influence is legitimate, whereas interference is not. This distinction was neatly presented by the 2017 Foreign Policy White Paper, which stated:

> All states seek to advance their interests by persuading others to their point of view. This is a central and legitimate task of diplomacy. Foreign interference goes further by using clandestine or deceptive means to affect political, governmental or even commercial processes to cause harm to Australian interests.

When Prime Minister Malcolm Turnbull introduced legislation in 2017 to counter foreign interference, he also distinguished between influence and interference, which involves conduct that is "covert, coercive or corrupt".

Such a distinct line meant that many of the PRC's influencing activities are not captured by the legislation. ANU senior fellow Katherine Mansted made the case in 2021 that the divide between influence and interference is unhelpful, as the PRC has adopted strategies that "exploit the grey zone between acceptable foreign influence activities and unlawful foreign interference".

When it comes to media reporting and public perceptions, however, the distinction between influence and interference is blurred. Media organisations lump together different stories to do with the PRC under the banner of "Chinese influence". Attempts to influence are often portrayed as illegitimate and malign if there are "links" or "connections" to the PRC. The participation of PRC students in student politics, for example, was characterised by the ABC's *Four Corners* in 2019 as "a gateway for CCP influence on campus". Yet the fundamental principle of freedom of speech requires that PRC citizens should be able to advocate for their political views peacefully, regardless of whether those views are pro-PRC or not.

The federal government has not done enough to clarify this confusion between influence and interference, and many experts appear to have wittingly ignored the reality that foreign influence is a legitimate part of a liberal democracy.

Australia allows dissenting voices to be heard. Authoritarian countries such as the PRC do not. As a result, the PRC is subject to significantly less foreign influence. The PRC government is hypersensitive to any "hostile foreign forces" and blames them for many of its domestic troubles. That is the primary reason behind the crackdown on civil rights groups such as LGBTIQA+ groups, which are presented as national security threats. Eliminating foreign influence and blaming foreign forces for dissent would move Australia closer to an authoritarian model and betray our democratic ideals.

Selective enforcement and racial profiling

Since the PRC does not allow "hostile foreign forces", should Australia reciprocate? Many Australians believe the answer should be yes, and that Australia should restrict foreign influence activities by the PRC. Yet such an approach would make Australia more like the PRC.

Proponents of such reciprocity take issue with the country-agnostic nature of the foreign interference legislation. While introducing the legislation, Turnbull emphasised that "interference is unacceptable from any country whether you might think of it as friend, foe or ally".

The legislation established the Foreign Influence Transparency Scheme, to provide the public with visibility of foreign influence on Australia's government and politics. Most of the activities listed on the register were undertaken on behalf of Australia's friends rather than the PRC, presumably because those organisations are more likely to comply. But the revelation prompted some national security experts to argue for abandoning the country-agnostic principle. Daniel Ward, former general counsel to Prime Minister Scott Morrison, proposed in 2021 that "Australia's foreign influence laws should be amended to adopt a 'tiered model', under which conduct originating in certain 'designated countries' would be subject to greater regulation than activity from other sources".

In any case, country-agnostic legislation does not guarantee that all countries or individuals are treated the same. The *Immigration Restriction Act 1901*, which was the cornerstone of the White Australia policy, was country-agnostic. It gave officials the discretion to restrict individuals from entering Australia, but mentioned no race or country in particular. Instead, any migrant could be required to take a dictation test. The effect, of course, was that non-Europeans were excluded.

Attempts to influence are not restricted to authoritarian countries

Government agencies have a choice about which foreign interference investigations to pursue, and which to make public. Intelligence agencies can investigate instances of influence from one country (if it is perceived as malign), while ignoring influence from another (if it is supposedly benign).

Selective enforcement was apparent in the now-defunct "China Initiative" in the United States. An attempt to target the PRC's theft of trade secrets led to the prosecution of Chinese Canadian scientist Anming Hu in 2011. While investigating him for espionage, a team of FBI agents tailed his family for two years. They placed him on the no-fly list and got him fired based on false information, and even pressured him to spy for the US government. And despite finding no evidence of espionage, the US government charged him with fraud. Hu was eventually acquitted, but lost two years of his life to this fiasco.

The criteria for investigations under the China Initiative – which the Department of Justice ended in 2022 – was that the activities had "some nexus" to the PRC. It was therefore a strictly state-based rather than race-based criteria. Yet the implementation led to extensive racial profiling, targeting Chinese and Chinese American scholars.

This is not to say that foreign interference investigations are racist. Far from it – there are many legitimate interference concerns. However, if investigations only focus on interference from the PRC, then people with links to the PRC will be unduly targeted. And most of these people will be of Chinese heritage.

Targets are not always agents

While the CCP would prefer that all its influencing attempts are successful and all its targets become its agents, this is certainly not the case.

The party attempts to influence individuals and organisations in the Chinese diaspora in Australia and other countries through its United Front Work Department, which aims to strengthen the party's legitimacy by co-opting those outside the party. However, an individual or organisation is not necessarily an agent purely because they have been targeted by the PRC. Similarly, sharing the same view as the PRC on certain issues is not evidence that a person is an agent of the PRC. Extraordinary accusations, such as that of foreign interference, require proof, not just circumstantial innuendo.

Perhaps it is worth pausing to consider why a certain segment of the Australian public is so easily persuaded that targets of PRC influence activities are agents, especially when they are ethnic Chinese. According to the 2023 UTS:ACRI/BIDA poll, which explores "Australian views on the Australia–China relationship", 43 per cent of Australians believe that "Australians of Chinese origin can be mobilised by the Chinese government to undermine Australia's interests and social cohesion".

There is an undercurrent of belief that people of Chinese ethnicity will naturally be loyal to the PRC, and thus are susceptible to becoming its agents. This is why we saw the Australian Senate asking Chinese Australians to demonstrate their loyalty to Australia by condemning the Chinese Communist Party.

This belief stems partly from a racist impression that ethnic Chinese people have been brainwashed and are incapable of independent thought. In fact, most PRC international students and migrants are not supportive of every PRC policy. Even inside the PRC there exists a push for more rights, despite harsh censorship and crackdowns. Yet the same people who are pushing for these changes might back the Chinese government on other issues, such as the territorial dispute over the South China Sea. Just like people everywhere, PRC citizens and Chinese Australians pursue their own beliefs and interests, rather than blindly following their governments' directives.

Politics for sale

In 2017, political donations by property developer Chau Chak Wing came under the spotlight. Media reports and Liberal Party MP Andrew Hastie – at the time the chair of the Parliamentary Joint Committee on Intelligence and Security, and the current Shadow Minister for Defence – suggested that Chau had used political donations to influence Australian government policy on behalf of the PRC. There is no doubt that he used donations to try to influence policy: this is what all political donors do. The critical question is whether he did so on behalf of the PRC, which remains without a conclusive answer.

The buying of influence through lobbying and political donations in a democracy has always been controversial but accepted, as long as it is openly declared. As the US political scientist Yuen Yuen Ang has pointed out, lobbying and donations are a form of access money – "high-stakes rewards offered by elite capitalists to powerful officials in exchange for exclusive, lucrative privileges". Although legal, they are a form of corruption. It is no wonder that wealthy companies and individuals take advantage of this to influence government policy.

Since foreign governments cannot easily donate to politicians, they attempt to influence policy through donations to think tanks. In the United States, for example, the Brookings Institution, a major think tank, allegedly lobbied the US government in 2017 on behalf of Qatar. This controversy led to the resignation of the president of Brookings, retired general John Allen. Such attempts to influence are not restricted to authoritarian countries. Norway and Japan are also in the influence game, donating millions to US think tanks with specific policy requests or research directions.

In Australia, foreign donations to political parties were banned in 2018 after the controversies with two donors associated with PRC influence, Chau Chak Wing and Huang Xiangmo. Yet neither was a foreign donor: one was an Australian citizen and one an Australian resident, so their donations would have been legal even under the new law.

> **An overreaction to foreign interference risks eroding ... freedom of speech**

With the sharp focus on how the PRC is taking advantage of Australia's democratic system, an opportunity is missed to have a national conversation on how to reduce the corrupting influence of money in politics more generally. For example, a cap on donations would reduce influence over policy by wealthy individuals or corporations, including foreign governments. Focusing on broader electoral reform in this way, rather than just on the PRC's influence activities, would strengthen Australia's democracy.

WeChat and TikTok

Democracies are increasingly scrutinising another area of political influence: social media. Again, the most effective approach would be to focus on the tools of influence rather than on a single culprit.

A study in 2019 found that YouTube's recommendation algorithm has funnelled viewers to alt-right videos. A study in 2021 found that Facebook is driving political polarisation and spreading misinformation in the United States. However, there is no evidence that YouTube or Facebook are following state directives in implementing their algorithms. Despite the clear concerns about how they operate, the Australian government has not made them subject to its foreign interference investigations.

On the other hand, two social media apps owned by PRC companies have been accused of potential interference: WeChat and TikTok. Senator James Paterson, the Shadow Minister for Home Affairs and a member of the Parliamentary Joint Committee on Intelligence and Security, has repeatedly called for a boycott or ban of the two apps in Australia.

WeChat is owned by Tencent and, in Australia, is used predominantly by migrants from the PRC. The app is subject to censorship and political surveillance. However, a study by Deakin University academic Fan Yang found that there was no evidence of PRC influence over WeChat Official Accounts (WOAs) during the 2019 Australian federal election.

Instead, she found that "the political opinions espoused in the widely read and locally influential accounts we studied tended to directly counter those published by CCP affiliated WOAs during the election campaign". A 2023 study by university academics Wanning Sun and Haiqing Yu found that WeChat is used for both democratising and anti-democratising purposes, just like other social media platforms.

TikTok is owned by ByteDance. It is a popular app among Australians aged under thirty-five and has a much broader reach than WeChat. A government review in 2020 found that it did not pose serious national security concerns.

The fear around the two PRC apps is mainly around what *could* happen if the PRC were to pressure their owners to spread disinformation and manipulate elections. Such fear stems from a general distrust of the PRC, and of any business or individual who might be influenced by the PRC. But this ignores the fact that foreign governments can directly pressure any social media company, regardless of the nationality of its ownership.

For example, the Indian government has successfully pressured Twitter to censor a BBC documentary and block the account of a Canadian politician. Ironically, because the PRC has blocked the use of US-based social media apps such as Twitter and Facebook in China, it has actually lost the ability to influence those companies. As a result, Meta (the owner of Facebook) is actively lobbying for a ban on TikTok in the United States and Australia, since it would benefit from a ban and stands to lose nothing in the PRC. Corporate competition has become intimately linked to national security.

The focus on the "Chineseness" of TikTok and WeChat means that the public discourse has shifted away from how to regulate disinformation on all social media apps. For example, Twitter and Facebook have both amplified pro-Russia disinformation, despite the fact they are US companies and under no pressure from the Russian government.

Their US ownership did not eliminate the risk that they might be the conduit of foreign interference.

Australians can choose to engage with legitimate social media platforms or not. Pre-emptively banning these apps because they could be used to shape public opinion on behalf of the PRC goes against Australia's liberal-democratic principles – and would mirror what is done in places like the PRC. The fear that foreign influence could infiltrate the Chinese population was the justification used by the PRC to erect the "Great Firewall", which blocks access to services such as Google, Facebook and Twitter. We should be cautious about taking the same authoritarian approach.

Freedom of speech

The Great Firewall was created to prevent people inside the PRC from being exposed to criticisms of the Chinese government and the CCP. This reflects the insecurity of the government – it worries that "foreign hostile forces" might foment anti-government unrest.

The Chinese government also attempts to suppress criticisms of it outside its borders in other ways. Scholars researching issues deemed "sensitive" by the PRC – such as human rights – and dissidents who have emigrated from the PRC are the primary targets of this form of interference.

One well-documented method is the threatening of dissidents' family members who reside in the PRC. The government persuades or coerces the family to put pressure on these dissidents. The dissidents therefore face a difficult choice if they wish to continue their activism: either they ignore the plight of their family members, who may face detention or harassment, or they cut off all contact with their family in order to protect them and remove the source of PRC leverage.

Another common method, if the targets are not PRC citizens, is visa denial. This applies in particular to scholars who need to conduct field-work to advance their research. The PRC prevents them from travelling to China as a punishment, encouraging self-censorship in the future.

Social media presents an added layer of risk. Anyone might upload photos of anti-PRC protestors, who can then be identified by the Chinese government. Those who have uploaded the photos might have done it at the direction of the government or of their own volition. They might even be praising and supporting the protestors.

Only the first of these methods is what might be called foreign interference, yet all three can lead to trouble for the individuals involved.

It is often hard to determine whether someone is acting at the direction of a foreign government. For example, a PRC student in Australia might participate voluntarily in pro-PRC protests because they support the PRC government's stance on a particular issue, or they might tear down flyers because they disagree with the views expressed. Such activity is not foreign interference unless it is being done at the direction of the PRC, but it may interfere with the rights of others to express their views. Similarly, those who troll or harass others online are not necessarily agents of foreign interference, although this does not make their actions less concerning.

There is a dangerous tendency to label any activities perceived as pro-PRC as potential interference, and anyone who participates in those activities as a potential agent. In the absence of evidence, such accusations lead to self-censorship. An overreaction to foreign interference risks eroding the very right – to freedom of speech – that the foreign interference is seeking to undermine.

Freedom of association

It is a fact of life that when you engage with the PRC, you inevitably have to engage with the Chinese Communist Party. Approximately one in every fifteen people in the PRC – more than 96 million people – are Party members, and the figure is much higher among men with academic degrees. The doctor who blew the whistle on the spread of COVID-19 in Wuhan, Li Wenliang, was a member of the party. When an Australian prime minister meets with their PRC counterpart, they are meeting with the head of the CCP. And if you meet a person from the PRC – someone like me – the chances are good that someone from their extended family is a member of the Party.

The CCP is not a terrorist organisation under Australian law. It is not illegal to be a member of the Party, or to receive training, funding or other support from the Party. It is certainly not nefarious to shake hands or have your photo taken with a member of the Party. Indeed, if you are trying to get something done in or with the PRC and you are not talking to the Party, you are doing something seriously wrong.

Yet the CCP and its members have been portrayed in the Australian media as sinister, creating an impression that Australians should refrain from engaging with any CCP organisation or individual. For example, when accusing Chau Chak Wing of foreign interference, Andrew Hastie used Chau's "extensive contacts in the Chinese Communist Party" as a reason. Perhaps it will surprise Hastie to know that the Australian embassy in Beijing and most Australian businesspeople in the PRC also have "extensive contacts in the Chinese Communist Party".

In Australia, this fear of engagement with the CCP has led to scrutiny of some community organisations, particularly of United Front–affiliated community organisations in Australia. As discussed above, these organisations are usually the *targets* of the CCP's influencing attempts and are not necessarily its agents. Andrew Chubb has pointed out that "the co-optation strategy behind the CCP's United Front work is premised on an assumption that the 'patriotic' groups targeted are not inherently loyal to the CCP ... [but] pursue their own interests".

Anyone connected to the PRC doing anything political is suspected of foreign interference

Freedom of association is a basic right in a liberal democracy. In Australia, groups can choose to associate with foreign governments or embassies and receive funding from them. Many community groups in Canberra receive sponsorships from foreign embassies for events they hold. These embassy-sponsored events make Canberra a more vibrant place to live. The Canberra Diplomatic Club, for example, hosts networking events for diplomats and public servants, thus actively fostering foreign influence. All its monthly events are sponsored by embassies.

As it is difficult to prove "non-association", a guilty-until-proven-innocent mindset has emerged. For example, in 2021, the University of Sydney began to require its students, who have no access to classified information, to complete security clearance–like questionnaires. An overblown fear of being seen with United Front–affiliated groups and individuals has, in the past, led to several political candidates avoiding Chinese Australian community groups altogether.

Having links or associations with the CCP is in itself neither nefarious nor evidence of foreign interference. Yet in the last five years, it has often been used to smear others.

Media hysteria

Remember Wang Liqiang, the "Chinese spy" from *60 Minutes* in 2019? For a while, his face was plastered everywhere on television and on Nine's news websites. Wang alleged that he had worked for the PRC government on foreign interference operations. Andrew Hastie praised his courage, calling him a "friend of democracy". To many, that's where the story ended, and his claims were accepted as truth.

In fact, his story was later thoroughly discredited. In 2021 authorities in Taiwan found no evidence to support his claims, and in 2022 Australian authorities found that "based on a totality of inconsistencies, implausibility, admissions of forgery/procuring false documents and a history of lying, [Wang's] credibility is for the most part, unreliable". His bid for asylum in Australia was rejected. Yet these follow-ups received minimal media coverage. In the minds of most people, he was still the Chinese spy exposing the PRC's interference operations.

Media organisations in Australia have taken the credit for shining a spotlight on "Chinese influence". As a result, the Australian population has become more aware of activities linked to "foreign interference", such as political lobbying and the suppression of dissidents. However, at the same time, an overreaction has created an environment in which anyone connected to the PRC doing anything political is suspected of foreign interference.

Media stories have presented photos of politicians or political advisers meeting United Front Work Department officials as evidence of possible interference. In doing so, they deliberately mischaracterise attempts to influence as successful interference.

At the more extreme end, media outlets have engaged in overt race-baiting. A *Daily Mail Australia* news article from March 2023 accused three Chinese men of spying at the Avalon Airshow, an event open to the public. Their evidence? They looked Chinese and they had large cameras. The article quoted a "national security expert" who was "preparing a report for the Defence Department". *Daily Mail Australia* later withdrew the story without explanation.

As the Wang Liqiang episode shows, accountability is often missing in the Australian media's coverage of foreign interference. Despite the oft-repeated claims that the media is "shining light on hidden influences", reporters often rely on exclusive access to anonymous national security officials. The problem with this is that the media risks disseminating propaganda rather than holding the government to account.

Faith in democracy

I'm no longer a card-carrying member of the CCP's Young Pioneers. If the regrettable price of having a voice in the China debate is full disclosure of one's family and history, I have now paid my dues. I didn't flee the PRC as a political dissident. A far less dramatic thing happened: I became an Australian. Like many Australians, I now participate in the tradition of critiquing my government, in the hope that my voice will lift the quality of our public debate.

The public discourse on foreign influence and interference in Australia has had a significant impact on its democracy and values. The portrayal of Chinese Australians as easily manipulated by the PRC government to interfere in Australia betrays a fundamental lack of confidence in Australia's liberal democracy.

Chinese Australians, who comprise more than 5 per cent of Australia's population, have come under increasing scrutiny and suspicion due to their ethnic background. Many have started to self-censor and avoid expressing their views publicly for fear of being labelled a foreign agent. The racism this issue has inflamed has affected Asian Australians more broadly, with even Korean Australians accused of being "Chinese spies".

Yet these experiences are not usually considered when national security experts – most of whom are not from a diverse cultural background – discuss foreign interference. Implicitly, this shows that, to many of them, the racism Chinese Australians experience as a result is acceptable collateral damage.

What this means is that Chinese Australian voices are usually missing – both in public and within the government – in our policy debate about the PRC, including on foreign interference. This lack of diversity leads to a higher likelihood of groupthink. It is especially problematic as Chinese Australians are more likely to possess valuable China knowledge – an understanding of PRC politics, government, history and culture.

Fear of spurious interference accusations has led many to be wary of engaging in dialogues, exchanges or private diplomatic initiatives with the PRC. This serves to entrench the status quo. If Australians' participation in the Young Leadership Dialogue with the United States is celebrated and supported, while participation in similar dialogue with the PRC is seen as suspicious and detrimental to one's career, then the future relationship between Australia and the PRC will inevitably be affected.

When combating foreign interference, social cohesion is an asset – it should not be seen as a distraction. People in the Chinese Australian community (and others) want to be protected both from foreign interference as well as from spurious accusations and suspicions.

The Australian government must do more to distinguish between legitimate influence and unacceptable interference, and educate the public better by outlining concrete examples of both. It should reassure and support members of the Chinese Australian community about their legitimate engagement activities with the PRC government and people in the PRC.

The CCP frequently accuses those who hold different views and those who interact regularly with foreigners of espionage and interference. Should we choose to become like that, or should we instead put confidence in our liberal democratic values? It is hardly a choice. When dealing with risks or threats from the PRC, Australia must avoid emulating it. ■

THE FIX
Solving Australia's foreign affairs challenges

—

Phil Orchard on Why Australia Should Condemn Russia's Illegal Transfers and Deportations

"Australia could not only act under domestic law to target people involved in the deportations and transfers, but also coordinate this action with other states ... that have passed Magnitsky laws."

....

THE PROBLEM: When the International Criminal Court issued an arrest warrant for Russian president Vladimir Putin in March 2023, it was not for the invasion of Ukraine, or even for the wide range of war crimes allegedly committed by Russian soldiers. Instead, it was for his alleged responsibility in the unlawful transfer and deportation of children from occupied areas of Ukraine to Russia. (The court also issued an arrest warrant for Maria Lvova-Belova, the Russian Commissioner for Children's Rights.) This is a growing problem: the Ukrainian government has reported that (as of 24 August 2023) some

19,546 children have been deported into Russia. The Organization for Security and Co-operation in Europe (OSCE) has found that many of these so-called evacuations were "non-consensual" and "in certain cases … war crimes".

But these children are only part of a much larger forced movement of Ukrainians from occupied territory into Russia. While the full scope of these movements is unclear, up to August 2022 TASS, the Russian news service, was regularly reporting "evacuations" from Ukraine, figures that reached some 3.6 million. In July 2022, the United States estimated that Russian authorities had forcibly deported between 900,000 and 1.6 million Ukrainians, including 260,000 children. An inquiry set up by the United Nations concluded in March 2023 that these deportations also constitute a war crime.

These people are not just being forcibly moved, but are put through a traumatic "filtration" process by Russian authorities. It is common for parents and children to be separated; victims of the process have said they were subject to beatings and torture that might last weeks. Those who pass are then transported to Russia. But it is worse for those who do not. These people, numbering in the thousands, are detained in facilities inside Russian-controlled Donetsk. There have been unconfirmed reports of murders. The US ambassador to the OSCE reported that a witness overheard a conversation between two Russian soldiers. One asked the other: "What did you do with people who didn't pass the filtration?" The response: "Shot ten and stopped counting." Yale's Humanitarian Research Lab, which has closely studied the filtration process, has identified areas with disturbed earth outside one centre that had the visual characteristics of individual or mass graves.

Russia's deportation campaign is a clear violation of international law – not only war crimes, but also crimes against humanity. And the transfer of children is defined explicitly as a form of genocide under the 1948 Genocide Convention. But with Russia wielding power of veto in the United Nations Security Council, the Council has been unable to act.

Yet other options are available for states, including Australia, that want to try to prevent and punish these atrocities.

THE PROPOSAL: Australia can take action through two steps. The first is at the domestic level. In December 2021, Australia amended its *Autonomous Sanctions Act* to allow individuals to be sanctioned for serious violations of human rights, including "cruel, inhuman or degrading treatment or punishment". Such restrictions are widely referred to as "Magnitsky laws", named for Russian auditor Sergei Magnitsky, who died in prison in Russia for exposing government misconduct and corruption.

While Australia has applied Magnitsky sanctions against Russians involved in the death of Magnitsky and in the attempted assassination in 2020 of Russian opposition leader Alexei Navalny, we have not yet used them against those Russians involved in forcible deportations or in wider rights violations in Ukraine. In contrast, the US Treasury Department sanctioned three Russian officials and one member of the Donetsk People's Republic for their involvement in the filtration operations. The European Union sanctioned the head of Russia's Border Service for his involvement in "systematic 'filtration' operations and forced deportations of Ukrainians".

These types of sanctions work best when coordinated between different states. But, so far, no other states with Magnitsky laws have followed the United States and European Union, and no other sanctions have been applied since the arrest warrants were issued in March. Australia could not only act under domestic law to target people involved in the deportations and transfers, but also coordinate this action with other states – such as Canada and the United Kingdom – that have passed Magnitsky laws.

The second step would be to push for a United Nations General Assembly resolution condemning Russia's campaign of deportations and transfers of children. The General Assembly has actually been quite active on the Ukraine War. It has passed six resolutions against Russia, including a demand that Russian forces withdraw from Ukraine and a statement that Russia's attempts to annex four Ukrainian regions had no validity. Resolutions have also focused on the need to protect civilians and condemned violations of human rights.

But there does appear to be an appetite for more. A resolution passed in March 2022 demanded that all civilians fleeing the conflict be allowed "voluntary, safe and unhindered passage". Many nations have made statements opposing the deportation campaign, and highlighted the fact that it involves children. In May 2023, the G7 "strongly" condemned the deportations, and the newly released *Report on Children and Armed Conflict* by Secretary-General António Guterres noted that he was "appalled by the high number of grave violations against children in Ukraine following the invasion of Ukraine by the Russian Federation". That report could be used as a point of leverage for Australia to work with other countries to propose a General Assembly resolution condemning Russia's deportation campaign.

Australia can propose a resolution by itself, but, given the widespread concerns over Russia's conduct, a better step would be for our Permanent Mission to the United Nations to first line up a wide range of co-sponsors, particularly from the Global South. Such diplomacy could also support Australia's longer-term ambitions for a Security Council seat in 2029.

WHY IT WILL WORK: These might seem like small steps – and, yes, they are unlikely to cause Russia to immediately stop its illegal campaign. But small steps can have significant effects. First, they would raise the profile of the issue and might undermine Russia's attempts to avoid criticism. In this case, Moscow has appeared to be on the defensive. For instance, Lvova-Belova held a press conference following her arrest warrant being issued in which she defended Russia's actions, arguing that her commission was acting "on humanitarian grounds" to protect the children, and – in spite of clear evidence to the contrary – that it always seeks parental consent and does not give up children to adoption.

Further action would force Russia to respond. As US secretary of state Antony Blinken noted in a speech in June 2023, "Each rebuke and loss for Moscow is not only a vote against Russia's aggression, it's a vote for the core principles of the United Nations Charter. And countries from every part of the world are supporting efforts to hold Russia accountable for its war crimes and crimes against humanity …" Magnitsky sanctions would also signal to the lower-level Russian bureaucrats who administer these programs that their acts are illegal in international law, and that the international community is watching and willing to prosecute. This too creates a powerful deterrent effect.

Action at the General Assembly reinforces the strong global outrage against Russia (most resolutions pass with strong majorities, and with only between five and fourteen states voting against them). While these efforts would mirror those of states from the Global North, Australia's voice would play an important role with respect to the Global South and particularly the Asia-Pacific. Few states have so far adopted direct sanctions against Russia (Singapore, for instance, is the only ASEAN country to have done so).

Combined, these actions will, at the least, warn those involved in these deportations that they are being watched and might well face court. At best, they will lead to a shift in Russia's policies, a shift that could return these children to their distraught parents.

THE RESPONSE: The Department of Foreign Affairs and Trade said Australia had co-sponsored and voted for the six UN General Assembly resolutions condemning Russia and its invasion of Ukraine, including one calling for the return of those "forcibly transferred and deported, including children". Australia also joined forty-two states in referring the situation to the International Criminal Court, provided $1 million and three staff to support the court's investigation, and imposed sanctions and travel bans on Putin and Lvova-Belova.

"We are deeply concerned by evidence that Russia is deporting and adopting Ukrainian children into Russian families," said a spokesperson for the department. "Consistent with longstanding policy, the government does not speculate publicly on potential future sanctions." ■

Reviews

War on Corruption: An Indonesian Experience

Todung Mulya Lubis

Melbourne University Press

While Todung Mulya Lubis might not be a familiar name to most readers of Australian Foreign Affairs, he should be. An advocate, writer and pro-democracy rabble-rouser, Mulya has spent a lifetime advocating for a legal system that advances social equality, human rights and human dignity. That commitment has placed him at the forefront of Indonesia's vibrant democracy movement, building important institutions, from the nation's vital national legal aid network to Kontras (Commission for the Disappeared and Victims of Violence), a regional leader in its field. Mulya's fearless dedication to human dignity also brought him to defend two of Australia's "Bali Nine", Andrew Chan and Myuran Sukumaran, who were sentenced to death in 2006 for heroin smuggling. When they were executed by firing squad on 29 April 2015, Mulya tweeted desolately into the night, "I failed. I lost. I am sorry" and hundreds of tweets bearing Australian flags grieved alongside him.

Mulya's new book, *War on Corruption: An Indonesian Experience*, is a window onto his struggle against that other great injustice, corruption. Indonesian corruption, he argues, not only involves breaking the law and personal enrichment but has denied generations of Indonesians their rightful share in the country's social and economic development. Its roots go way back. In 1965, Suharto came to power promising a "New Order", in which the corruption of the old would be driven out. And yet Suharto would go on to establish a regime of corruption so entrenched that *Time* famously referred to it as "Suharto Inc.". In thirty-two years of rule, Suharto allegedly siphoned off between US$5 billion and US$35 billion from the public purse, much of it through a network of companies owned by his family members. In 2000, Mulya defended *Time* from the Suharto family's lawsuit, but the book is oddly thin-lipped about the pressure he would have been under in defending public-interest journalism, or the way that, nine years later, his hard-won victory would finally set the record straight on over three decades of craven misrule.

While the Suharto regime fell in May 1998 to mass outrage about *"korupsi, kolusi dan nepotisme"* (corruption, collusion and nepotism), Mulya is the first to admit that the *Reformasi* (Reform) era he fought so bravely to realise has not lived up to expectations. He lays the blame on two of Indonesia's post–New Order institutions. First, he argues that political decentralisation and the swathe of opportunities opened up by fiscal devolution and local elections have been seized by local dynasties. By way of example, Lubis introduces us to "Ratu [Queen] Atut" of Banten, a province that makes up Jakarta's western industrial belt, who established a web of companies to reap the benefits of procurement

deals ordered by members of her vast family of local politicians and bureaucrats. Legally complex as that scheme was, the model was a provincial replica of Suharto Inc. If democracy was her opening, it was also her downfall. Atut's candidates lost a key election and she was ultimately imprisoned for corruption in 2014 when caught bribing the head of the Constitutional Court to announce a do-over that would swing the election result in her favour.

An even bigger source of blame is Indonesia's political party system, which over twenty years of democratic elections has been whittled down to nine national parties, which, Mulya points out, are either dynasties or oligarchies, deeply embedded in the country's richest families and conglomerates. As Indonesia inches towards a national and presidential election early next year, Mulya reminds us that political parties are seeking to "capture" Indonesia's state institutions, securing positions and authorities that will allow them to siphon funds into their coffers for electoral campaigning. While illicit party financing arguably exists across the political spectrum, the current ruling party, the Indonesian Democratic Party of Struggle (PDI-P), has intensified this model of institutional capture to a shocking degree of brazenness. The coming year will test whether the PDI-P's brand of hyper-predation will translate into electoral success.

Mulya's analysis of corruption also invites discussion of Indonesia's historical responses to combat it. Yet Mulya ignores the wildly popular social movements, non-governmental organisations and other civil society institutions that strive to expose wrongdoing and support anti-corruption reformers – a struggle in which he himself was so instrumental. Instead, Mulya takes us on a tour of the various institutional innovations that different political regimes have instigated to curtail corruption.

The most important of these, the Corruption Eradication Commission (KPK), was formed in 2002, in the heyday of the *Reformasi* movement. Over recent decades, Australian tax dollars have been put to good use consolidating this agency's powers. Modelled on the Hong Kong anti-corruption commission, the KPK went from a fledgling agency to an awesome and often controversial

"super-body" that took some major political scalps, from the head of the Constitutional Court to powerful ministers and governors. Much of the KPK's capacity rested on its alternative hiring and renumeration practices, which were deliberately set apart from the rest of the state bureaucracy, in addition to a host of administrative practices and investigative powers that guarded the agency's independence. Over time, the KPK was able to develop, train and retain a unique cohort of investigators, prosecutors, administrators and legal minds who relished the opportunity do meaningful work that served the nation; for some, it even bordered on the sacred.

The effects of the KPK on corruption patterns in the short term were, frankly, perverse. Corruption schemes became highly sophisticated, drawing in ever-widening domestic and transnational networks of associates, lawyers, accountants and "grey area" professional enablers to construct and conceal their architecture. In the long term, however, the KPK picked its cases from such a smorgasbord of political affiliations that the agency became a victim of its own success, effectively consolidating against it a grand coalition of parties, political brokers, conglomerates and religious organisations, which tried repeatedly to kneecap the agency's workings. Those efforts finally came to fruition in amendments to the original legislation, passed on the sly in September 2019.

Mulya is vehemently critical of the KPK reforms, forensically pulling apart the legislative articles designed to hobble its independence and authority. But, again, he is strangely silent about the specific political elites who pursued them – a repeat weakness that limits the book's critical approach. Mulya even drops

an odd confidence from President Jokowi himself, who, Mulya assures us, never meant to handicap the KPK. Mulya is also mum on the alliance of activists, students and civil society organisations who took to the streets to protest and yet were met with such violence, repression and digital harassment that the street-based movements that birthed the reform era, like the KPK itself, are now deeply debilitated. Facing the 2024 elections, the so-called Indonesian "war on corruption", as well as the progressive forces who made it seemingly so successful, are limping and battle-weary.

Jacqui Baker

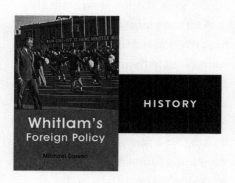

HISTORY

Whitlam's Foreign Policy
Michael Easson

Whitlam's Foreign Policy
Michael Easson
Connor Court Publishing

The Australian political scientist Graham Little once developed a neat model of political leadership. Couched in psychoanalytic theory, it attempted to match the emotional needs of different voting groups with different types of leaders. To put it crudely, "group" leaders specialised in the politics of sympathy and compassion, "strong" leaders demanded loyalty in exchange for a robust defence of a group's interests, and "inspiring" leaders found a way to transcend the tension between the first two, shifting the boundaries of political possibility and forging new political solutions.

Little's categories still make for entertaining dinner-party arguments, some of them mapping tidily onto the current crop of Australian political leaders. But it is worth noting that he first conceived of his theory in the 1970s – a turbulent decade in both Australian and international politics – and his examples were all politicians of that era. The classic Australian group leader, he thought, was Jim Cairns. The most obvious strong leader was Malcolm Fraser. And the prototypical inspiring leader, breaking through the political quagmire, was Gough Whitlam.

In the years since, this image of Whitlam as a political visionary has remained dominant. For the dewy-eyed Whitlamites, there was something different about his government, some nobility or higher purpose, "a certain grandeur" (as his speechwriter Graham Freudenberg later put it) that transcended the chaos of the time, making it more than a mere collection of policies and reforms. It was as if, per Graham Little, Whitlam embodied a change that was more psychological than material, the fulfilment of an intense emotional need among Australians desperate for new ways of thinking.

In *Whitlam's Foreign Policy*, the businessman, former trade union official and self-described dewy-eyed Whitlamite Michael Easson attempts to put the legend to one side, and to instead look "objectively" at Whitlam's most significant interventions in the international arena. In ninety-three brisk pages, sourced largely from existing historical scholarship, he provides potted summaries and brief assessments of the Labor leader's many foreign policy achievements, failures and controversies. The question at the heart of this essay-length book, though, is one that all of Whitlam's most ardent followers have likely asked themselves at some point in their lives: was this government really as transformative as it seemed at the time?

The obvious place to start looking for an answer to that question is China. Whitlam's visit to Peking as Opposition leader in July 1971 was fortuitously timed, anticipating a sudden and dramatic change in American policy by just a few days. But it was also principled, brave and prescient, symbolically sweeping the broom through decades of Cold War thinking and laying the foundations for one of Australia's most important and consequential relationships in the decades to come. Once in government, Whitlam moved quickly to offer China full diplomatic recognition, along with several other states, including East Germany and North Korea.

In international affairs, as with domestic policy, the Whitlam government was energetic and innovative. It pursued full independence for Papua New Guinea, brought France before the International Court of Justice over nuclear testing in the Pacific and announced an official end to the White Australia policy. After an initial period of intense hostility with Washington over its criticism of aggressive American actions in Vietnam, it also largely put to bed American reservations about Labor's commitment to the alliance, and renegotiated agreements over joint defence facilities on the Australian mainland.

Whitlam was at pains to point out that his was not a radical overhaul of Australia's approach to international relations. His government, he said, continued to receive largely the same advice as its predecessors. Rather, like a lot of foreign policy shifts, his were mostly changes of emphasis: a little less on great-power relationships, a little more on regional ties and international bodies. Easson largely agrees, arguing that Whitlam's policies were an "untidy mix of perspectives, policy positions and priorities".

For every achievement, though, there was a failure or a controversy. Whitlam, Easson contends, was an "old fashioned liberal intellectual" with a lawyerly belief in the efficacy of argument and a slight deafness to the kinds of linguistic nuance that carry so much weight in international affairs. His declared policy of even-handedness on the highly sensitive Arab–Israeli dispute, for example, often felt like anything but, especially when he spoke of "secure borders" or made references to "the legitimate rights of the Palestinian people". "Meaning inheres in language," writes Easson, and, by his reckoning, Whitlam often failed this test of diplomatic delicacy.

Whitlam also sought closer relations with Indonesia, visiting three time as Opposition leader and twice more as prime minister, as well as hosting President Suharto in Townsville in 1975. But when Portugal suddenly abandoned its colonial interests in East Timor in 1974 and the island descended into civil war, Whitlam was left between a rock and a hard place, unsure whether to support the territorial claims of Australia's largest neighbour or to back a nascent East Timorese independence movement. Of all the blemishes on Whitlam's foreign policy record, Easson suggests, the subsequent humanitarian disaster in East Timor was the most disastrous.

Was there a guiding philosophy behind all this activity? Whitlam described himself as "idealistic, yet realistic", pursuing principled policies while remaining clear-eyed about the challenges Australia faced as a middle power in Asia. The Timor crisis was representative of his government's core dilemma, exposing the tension between its realism – its desire to foster close and stable relations with major powers – and its internationalism – its support for small state sovereignty, rights and institutions. As Easson puts it, "Whitlamism" in the international arena involved "seeking to do good while advancing the national interest".

One of Whitlam's goals was to shift Australian eyes towards Asia. In hindsight, the logic of this pivot can seem almost self-evident. By the time Labor came to government, many of the strategic and material props of the old policy consensus were gone. The British had announced the withdrawal of their military presence "East of Suez", and the Americans had signalled their intention to scale back their own military interventions in the region. By the mid-1960s, Japan had surpassed the United Kingdom as the largest market for Australian exports.

What remained in place, and what Whitlam sought to upend, were the psychological and sentimental attachments to the old order, the mental coordinates that were so deeply inscribed onto the minds of generations of Australian policymakers and political leaders: the idea that Australia should seek its security from Asia, not in it. All of Australia's postwar prime ministers anxiously grappled with this problem, and all tentatively experimented with solutions. But it was Whitlam who said it out loud, who told Australians where they were in the world and what that meant.

Whitlam's appeal, writes Easson, lay largely in "how he perceived the world". What made him so transformative – inspiring, even – were his confident proclamations about "what should and could be". Of all his foreign policy innovations, it is this attitudinal one that has had the biggest impact, his deliberate recalibration of Australia's mental compass in response to a changed and changing world. Just over fifty years since that first trip to China, it might be time for another.

Ryan Cropp

CAMBODIA

A Tiger Rules the Mountain: Cambodia's Pursuit of Democracy
Gordon Conochie
Monash University Publishing

Look back at the last four decades of Australian political leadership and count the names: the nation was led by Prime Minister Bob Hawke, then Paul Keating, John Howard, Kevin Rudd, Julia Gillard, Kevin Rudd again, Tony Abbott, Malcolm Turnbull, Scott Morrison and now Anthony Albanese. Cambodians do not need to count like that. The only prime minister Cambodia has known since 1985 is Hun Sen, who has ruled the country with an iron fist. He is the longest-serving ruler in Cambodia's modern history.

But this year, things have changed abruptly. After an uncontested election, Cambodia has welcomed a new prime minister. And there was no uncertainty about who it would be. In December 2021, Hun Sen publicly endorsed his eldest son, Hun Manet, to take over. He is the first Cambodian graduate from the United States Military Academy at West Point. Days after the 23 July national election, Hun Sen announced his resignation and set out a timeframe for appointing the new prime minister, with a passage through cabinet assured – even though the election result hadn't been finalised. His son will rule the country together with other sons and daughters of the old guard.

Before Hun Sen's era ended, Gordon Conochie wrote this important book covering the way the lives and souls of Cambodians were impacted by the regime, particularly during the last decades when the prime minister had a plan to "defend his mountain at all costs". *A Tiger Rules the Mountain* is a history of the final chapter of Hun Sen's era.

Conochie is an adjunct research fellow at La Trobe University and a former journalist. In Cambodia, he worked at the Ministry of Education and at UNICEF and the World Bank. In his book, readers travel with him from village to village to hear stories and voices from ordinary Cambodians, local politicians, eyewitness commentators and investigative journalists. They also hear from people involved in decision-making and democratic development, including members of the government, the opposition and international charities.

Divided into four parts, the book chronicles twists and turning points in Cambodian politics, which is as unpredictable as the character of the former prime minister. Each part is filled with Cambodian proverbs that define the cultural relationship between the ruled and the ruler. People who dare to break this custom pay a high price, as Kem Ley, the prominent commentator, discovered. An inspiration among Cambodian academics, Ley was gunned down in 2016 in the capital, Phnom Penh, in broad daylight in a service station where he regularly went for coffee. The man who shot him claimed his name was Choup Samlab ("Meet to Kill"), and he said he murdered Ley due to an unpaid debt. There was no further investigation, despite media reports revealing that the men had never met. Ley was shot just days after he gave an interview to Radio Free Asia concerning a Global Witness report on corruption involving Hun Sen and his family.

The ruling party consolidates power through a too-strong patronage system, nepotism, threats and intimidation of opponents and dissenters, and with China's backing. Those members of Cambodia's younger generation who stand up against it scramble, as the proverb puts it, like an "an egg hitting a stone" – a process that is well described in Part Two of Conochie's book.

What intrigued me most was the dialogue between the author and his sources. The conversations are frank and explicit, and illustrate people's political views honestly in an environment where free speech is regularly suppressed. Where views are implicit, the author gives cultural context and justification. Those stories will resonate with every Cambodian family.

I grew up as a "daddy's girl". I remember our family dinners well – there were five of us but the room was filled with only two voices, my father's and mine, as we argued about politics and society. My father is a government official and very savvy about the news. He has always wanted me to be well educated, to think critically and to "use knowledge to help our country's development". He thought I could achieve this only by following his path. His well-intentioned plan for me was to work in a government ministry, while I had a plan to escape.

I enrolled at a journalism school and became a journalist, a plan that I only revealed to my father on the day I broadcast my first story on one of Cambodia's independent radio stations, Voice of America. My father once claimed that when young people are educated, they "grow wings"; his comment, in the typically indirect Cambodian style, could suggest they gain liberation, or it could suggest betrayal. But, secretly, I know he is proud of me.

It is easy for the international community to think geopolitically about Cambodia. But Cambodians have stories, relating not only to their geographical sovereignty, and they want the international community to hear more from ordinary people, not just from the top 1 per cent. If the international community heard these stories, they would understand the complexities of Cambodian life and politics, and not just release a three-paragraph statement confirming what is already known: that the recent election was "neither free nor fair".

The international community can learn from the past when considering how to deal with a country that has such a close alliance with China. It can begin by looking back at the environment during the 2013 election, which was seen as "mostly free and fair", although it was not good enough. At that election, people were informed by an independent press and had a choice of candidates, and they positively believed in change – unlike at this year's election, when the government determined which party could be on the ballot.

It is too late to do anything about the latest election. The former prime minister already has a plan for his son, who is unlikely to escape it. Cambodians want to know who Hun Manet really is, and they hope his rule marks a positive change for the nation. He faces many challenges, including a debt crisis, systematic corruption, social injustice, economic impacts from the pandemic and democratic backsliding.

Conochie titles the final chapter of his book, which is actually Chapter 43, as "Chapter Two" of Cambodian politics as it undergoes a change of leader – a process that is so common elsewhere. With its wide-ranging interviews and intelligent observations about Cambodia at a crossroads, *A Tiger Rules the Mountain* is the best guide to the nation during this unusual time.

Sokummono Khan

Correspondence

"Target Australia"
by Sam Roggeveen

Luke Gosling

S am Roggeveen's "Target Australia" (Australian Foreign Affairs 18) argues that Australia's policy of deepening the US alliance is making us less safe in an era of growing competition with China. While others have expressed similar views, Roggeveen restates the case with admirable clarity and forcefulness. But questionable assumptions undermine his bleak conclusions about our alliance with America.

For one, Roggeveen assumes that, like an unquestioning deputy sheriff, Australia is choosing to be coopted into US military strategy at the expense of our decision-making autonomy. Thus, refurbishments enabling US bombers to operate from the Northern Territory "are effectively integrating RAAF Tindal into America's war planning". He implies that such moves, designed to deter war, are in fact increasing its likelihood – and constraining our options should one occur.

These alarming claims rest on a self-contradictory view of America's role in Asia. Roggeveen says the United States is bent on using Australia "to achieve regional dominance and defeat China in a war over Taiwan". Yet his America is also hesitant, risking "a retrenchment, of sorts" from Asia. Which is it? Roggeveen calls for the United States to be a regional "balancer", a role Foreign Minister Wong has also emphasised. Even if it wanted it, the US can't achieve regional hegemony, but it is strong enough to deny it to others. And that's in our interest.

At the heart of Roggeveen's analysis is the fear of Australia automatically entering a US-led war in the Indo-Pacific. "Simply having such a fleet will raise expectations in Washington that we would use it to help the United States in a war against China," he writes. Or again: "Having made that kind of investment [i.e. AUKUS], it seems unlikely that Australia would withhold it at the critical moment." Merely possessing SSN AUKUS boats, he argues, will tie our leaders' hands in a crisis.

But Australia is perfectly capable of saying no to America when it is in our interest, just as Labor said no to our great and powerful friend Britain's Singapore strategy, to sending the 7th Division to Burma instead of Australia in 1942, and to the US invasion of Iraq in 2003. Prime Minister John Curtin's statement that the "primary responsibility of any Australian Government [is] to ensure the security and integrity of its own soil" rings as true today. Any American administration would say the same.

Next, Roggeveen sees the alliance as yielding diminishing returns. Does it serve our interests, he asks, if the advanced capabilities we acquire through it lead to an "increased likelihood of Chinese military assault on Australia", incentivising a "pre-emptive surprise attack"? In his view, US bomber sorties from RAAF Tindal, an east-coast submarine base, rotations of US and UK nuclear-powered submarines through HMAS Stirling, and possessing hypersonic missiles are escalatory and might be targeted by China, even by nuclear weapons, in a war.

Roggeveen's take on the security dilemma frames Australia's acquisition of long-range strike capabilities as making us a bigger target. Being able to strike targets on the Asian mainland to deter an adversary, he thinks, creates an escalatory cycle we cannot win. Alan Dupont has argued the other side of the coin: "Yes, we are a target. But that is the price we pay for our independence and sovereignty, as does any self-respecting country."

If Roggeveen is right, then maybe Australia should adopt what he has in other writings called an "echidna strategy": a "non-offensive force structure", renouncing the ability to strike long-range targets and learning to defend ourselves without US assistance. That could mean slowing or ceasing investments both in AUKUS (an internal balancing strategy) and in the US alliance (external balancing), in the hope that China will grow more benevolent towards our interests as the regional balance of power favours it even more.

But what if Roggeveen is wrong? In that case, limiting the Australian Defence Force's size, range and lethality in a small-target strategy could itself be the more dangerous policy. Keeping a low profile in the hope that not contributing to deterrence will prevent us from being targeted might work. Or it might fail catastrophically, and see us one day at war and having only a stunted force and disinterested allies. There is no guarantee that divesting from the US alliance and restraining the ADF's growth will keep us safe from attack.

Though critics may quibble with the fine print of ANZUS, the US alliance remains the second-best insurance policy against this risk, and a force maximiser for the most important one, the ADF. Australia remains a US ally not for sentimental reasons, but because it is a core national interest, independently of whether it also serves Washington's interests. We can ultimately agree that this should never pre-commit Australia to war, and that a sovereign decision can only to be taken in the interest of our "own soil".

Luke Gosling is the Member for Solomon and Co-Chair of the Parliamentary Friends of the United States and of the Parliamentary Friends of AUKUS groups.

William Leben

I n "Target Australia", Sam Roggeveen offers a useful provocation about the strategic choices Australia is making. For Roggeveen, we are not thinking enough about the latent nuclear risks in the region, and force posture changes linked to AUKUS make Australia more of a target. More importantly, he declares, the United States isn't really committed to the region, or at least to a potential war with China over Taiwan.

I share many of Roggeveen's concerns. Certainly, the absence of serious discussion in Australia about the risks of regional escalation is a problem. The level of literacy on these issues is low, even among relevant policymaking communities. This deficiency is pressing because of the kinds of military capability we are set to acquire.

But I am not sure Roggeveen is right on a number of the issues he raises, or that his eventual conclusion is consistent with his own declared worries.

First, he inaccurately characterises certain capability decisions. Most starkly, he states that "the requirement for the new submarines to carry Tomahawk cruise missiles can only be interpreted one way: Australia wants the capability to strike targets on Chinese soil". Clearly, this is a capability that could be used to strike targets on Chinese soil. But to state that this is the only rationale for such a capability decision is a substantial leap.

This is not a quibble over wording. Weapons with longer and longer ranges are now central to credible military force. Simplistically, this is because the proliferation of sensors and missiles has made most operating environments more lethal, and the need to be able to "stand off" from a target at great distance is critical. Roggeveen is an experienced analyst of these issues and must know this. Whether or not buying nuclear-powered submarines is a good decision, putting long-range strike weapons on what will be Australia's most survivable platform will have broad military utility.

Second, the handling of a range of escalation worries in "Target Australia" seems unfinished. This is understandable – we are all keeping to word counts, I appreciate – but some of this context really matters. Roggeveen is right that we need to think more seriously about the use of capabilities that could implicate Chinese nuclear weapons. But this is a choice about deployment, not the first and principal consideration about whether or not Australia should buy a capability.

Roggeveen is also right that it "is hard to overstate the sensitivity involved in threatening another nation's nuclear forces". But his focus on the small (though growing) state of China's nuclear arsenal and its potential vulnerability is odd. There is an absence of the most pressing questions about the nuclear balance. Is it possible, for example, for the United States to target Chinese command-and-control systems, which serve both conventional and nuclear forces, without triggering nuclear catastrophe? This is an urgent question that, with or without AUKUS, we should be worried about.

And what of other destabilising capabilities, like hypersonic weapons? Roggeveen points out that these are set to increase pre-emption pressures, because they potentially offer a potent, rapid offensive capability against which there is no defence. You might need to shoot first to have any chance of winning, simply because there will be no time to respond in the event you are attacked. But there is context missing here, too. China's test of a hypersonic capability in 2021 reportedly shocked many Western analysts, though we of course need to regard public assessments of US and Chinese capability developments sceptically. There does not appear to be much prospect of regulating or restricting these capabilities, though perhaps an opportunity will emerge in time. It seems unlikely that the risk can be managed from a position of weakness, by asking the other party to forgo a major advantage.

Third, and most seriously, the profound conclusion drawn by Roggeveen at the close of his essay seems incongruent with the analysis that precedes it. Or perhaps the problem is that he sidesteps his real conclusion.

In a two-step finale, we are told that "the US is drifting into a balance-of-power arrangement with China", but that this "presents an opportunity ... to bend American objectives towards a more achievable and stabilising role of balancer rather than leader".

For starters, it seems a large step to make the first statement based on what is essentially solely a military-strategic analysis. What of the *CHIPS Act*, for instance? We might worry about the state of the American polity, and about the implications of American war talk on China. But to blithely dismiss the remarkable bipartisan commitment in Washington to overt competition with China is a courageous analytic move.

Ultimately, it isn't clear, though, what would be different in military terms were US deployments to the region, including to Australia, in the service of "a more achievable and stabilising role". American bombers and attack submarines, which understandably concern Roggeveen, will be part of any American force projection in the broad region – not just a force fighting for Taiwan.

Roggeveen's real concern, then, is perhaps not about American military basing, or particular new Australian capabilities. It's about the United States' "strategy to fight China". But we get very little on what this actually means. Fighting over Taiwan is clearly a worry, but we are told that America is "inching" towards "giving up on defending Taiwan" anyway. So would a willingness to defend, say, Japan count? The Philippines? What about intervening in a crisis on the Korean Peninsula? Doing any of those things would involve large escalation risks.

So are we talking about American retrenchment from all of those contingencies, or from any military involvement in the Western Pacific? Is that the outcome that would be a "more justifiable basis on which the US could deploy forces to Australia"? Indeed, under such a retrenchment, one wonders whether there would be much American desire to deploy or base forces in Australia. Regardless: if this is the alternative that we might seek, if we cannot envision any way in which the escalation risks might acceptably be managed under the status quo, we ought to recognise the radical implications of this conclusion. This would not be an outcome confined to Taiwan, nor a glossed "more modest role" for the United States, it would be American absence as a major security partner through the region. Let us say what we mean.

William Leben is a senior research officer at the National Security College, ANU.

Margaret Beavis

n his insightful essay "Target Australia", Sam Roggeveen analyses Australia's decision to host US B-52 bombers and to acquire nuclear-powered submarines under the AUKUS agreement. Roggeveen asks a particularly poignant question: does this serve Australia's interests? He argues that these "fateful decisions" – instead of making us safer – will increase the likelihood of a Chinese assault on Australia, of a war with China escalating to nuclear war, and of our air or naval bases becoming nuclear targets.

There are many additional questions that need to be asked.

Will Australia's acquisition of nuclear-powered submarines (SSNs) worsen nuclear weapons proliferation globally? We will be the first country to exploit a loophole in the Non-Proliferation Treaty (NPT) in order to gain access to the material and technology as a non-nuclear-armed nation. UK and US submarines use highly enriched uranium (HEU), which can also be used in nuclear weapons.

Tariq Rauf, former Head of Verification at the International Atomic Energy Agency, noted that our acquisition could well open a Pandora's box. Non-nuclear-weapon states such as Argentina, Brazil, Canada, Iran, Japan, Saudi Arabia and South Korea are also proposing acquiring SSNs.

Australia's acquisition of HEU undermines Australia's own efforts to reduce HEU use and stocks, and to achieve a "fissile material cut-off treaty", something the government claims is still a priority.

Department of Foreign Affairs and Trade officials briefed foreign diplomats in March 2023, reassuring them that the AUKUS submarine plan is "difficult and expensive" and not "easy to replicate", as part of an effort to play down concerns about the risk of other countries racing to do the same. One has to ask: has any country's nuclear weapons program ever been easy, cheap or, for that matter, easy to replicate?

At this same meeting, diplomats were assured that "Australia was committed to setting the highest possible non-proliferation and safety standards, which other states bearing legitimate ambitions to acquire SSNs would similarly have to meet". This undertaking has already been breached, with the new nuclear safety regulator for the submarines planned to report to the defence minister – the main proponent of the project. If safety standards were really a priority, they would be regulated by the established and independent Australian Radiation Protection and Nuclear Safety Agency (ARPANSA).

The decision to acquire nuclear-powered submarines that are part of US war planning has already escalated tensions in our proudly nuclear-free Pacific region. Our neighbours, including Malaysia and Indonesia, have indicated their opposition, concerned that the program risks sparking a regional arms race.

As Roggeveen notes, the submarines are to be armed with US Tomahawk cruise missiles (which can carry conventional or nuclear payloads), indicating that "Australia wants the capability to strike targets on Chinese soil". In a conflict, there would always be ambiguity regarding what payload a missile carries, increasing the risk of nuclear weapons use due to misunderstanding or miscalculation.

A further question is the cost of the submarines. They will dominate Australian budgets for decades, stripping expenditure from other key areas. An acquisition this size is also likely to impede diplomatic efforts, overshadowing other priorities.

This is a very high-risk project for many reasons. In March 2023, an ANU report found that the oceans were "likely" or "very likely" to become "transparent" by the 2050s. This would dramatically reduce the effectiveness of submarines. Does Australia want to invest in a nuclear system whose use-by date might be much earlier than assumed? Another major risk is the multiple changes of government in Australia, in the United States and in the United Kingdom between now and any postulated delivery date.

Roggeveen observes that the proposed stationing of B-52 aircraft should have caused much more of a stir than it did, given they effectively integrate RAAF Base Tindal into America's war planning, enabling operational missions from Australian soil. Around half the deployed US fleet of B-52s were stripped of their capacity to carry nuclear weapons, in accordance with the 2010 New START treaty. To avoid ambiguity, Australia can and must specifically exclude nuclear-capable aircraft from Tindal.

Australia should support and not undermine nuclear non-proliferation and disarmament. It should ensure that the nuclear-powered submarines and the B-52 stationing do not become the thin end of the wedge for nuclear weapons hosting, delivery or acquisition by Australia. The most effective way to do this is for the Australian government to fulfil a policy commitment to join the UN Treaty on the Prohibition of Nuclear Weapons (TPNW).

Roggeveen is clearly concerned about the trade-offs that come with AUKUS. Our acquisition of future SSNs, hypersonic missiles, plus American bomber and SSN facilities will alter Chinese military calculations and erode crisis stability. Pre-emptive strikes are more likely, from either side. He also flags China possibly detonating a nuclear weapon in Australia to demonstrate resolve against the United States, while hoping to avoid full-scale nuclear war. The costs of AUKUS may well outweigh any benefits.

Roggeveen hopes that Australia can work "to bend American objectives towards a more achievable and stabilising role of balancer rather than leader". Australia can also enhance global security by joining the ninety-two countries that have signed the TPNW. As the first of the "nuclear umbrella" states to sign, it would send a strong signal – and legally bind the present and all future Australian governments – not to acquire, host, deliver or assist with nuclear weapons. Such a decision would be a proud legacy for this government. These weapons are not acceptable in any hands, under any circumstances, and must be eliminated.

Margaret Beavis is Co-Chair of ICAN Australia.

Wesley Morgan

Even if everything goes according to plan, Australia won't build its first AUKUS submarines until 2040 at the earliest. By then we'll be spending a lot more time worrying about the world's oceans than about the submarines in them. As UN Secretary-General António Guterres says, we have already entered a new era of "global boiling", driven by our continued use of fossil fuels. Around 93 per cent of the world's excess heat is held by the ocean, which today absorbs excess energy at a rate equivalent to five Hiroshima bombs a second.

Mid-century threat assessments that focus only on the distribution of military power ignore the most serious security challenge of our time: the prospect of catastrophic climate change. Severe impacts – such as from sea-level rise and flooding, stronger storms and wildfires – are already being felt everywhere from New York to Shanghai, Sydney to the South China Sea. As these impacts worsen, societies will be reshaped. With each new increment of heating, we will move closer to irreversible tipping points in the Earth's climate system: the loss of sea ice, the melting of the Greenland ice sheet, the collapse of ocean currents. Everything depends on decisions made today. The stakes could not be higher.

Of course, Sam Roggeveen's essay is focused on submarines. It would be unfair to criticise it for setting to one side the warming oceans and climate-related threats that will frame all mid-century security concerns in the Indo-Pacific. Roggeveen argues that throwing our lot in with the United States' grand strategy in the region, by committing to a fleet of nuclear-powered submarines, will make Australia less safe by raising the risk of being dragged into a US–China war, which might not be central to our interests, could go nuclear and might have uncertain prospects of a US victory.

Australia has long made the calculation that aligning with a major power is key to our security: Britain before World War II, the United States since. But that does not mean we should blindly follow our "great and powerful friends". Roggeveen is right when he suggests Australia should aim to "bend American objectives" towards a stabilising role as regional balancer rather than as leader.

Australia should seek to bend American strategy in other ways as well. The Australia–US alliance was not established with a heating planet in mind, yet it must be reshaped to address that threat. In May 2023, Prime Minister Albanese and President Biden declared climate action a third pillar of the alliance, alongside defence and economic cooperation. This would have been bigger news had the announcement been made to a joint sitting of parliament, but Biden's visit to Canberra was scuttled by machinations over the US debt ceiling.

Recognising the threat is only the first step. Australia and the United States still need to develop a shared response. This includes integrating climate change into joint posture and strategic planning, to ensure the American and Australian militaries can respond to large-scale disasters and operate in more hostile conditions. More fundamentally, both nations will need to deploy all the instruments of statecraft to accelerate global efforts to cut greenhouse-gas emissions.

At home, both Australia and the United States will need to accelerate the shift away from fossil fuels and to clean energy technologies. This includes ending coal-fired power, moving beyond gas and investing in the infrastructure required for renewable energy. It also requires rethinking personal transport and decarbonising heavy industries such as steel and cement. If Australia can make a generational investment to build nuclear-powered submarines, committing $360 billion and developing the industrial capacity required, then similar commitments can be made to accelerate our shift away from fossil fuels, to ensure Australia's future as a clean energy powerhouse.

Australia and the United States will also need to cooperate to manage the global energy transition – a shift that will have profound strategic implications. Power is likely to move from 'petrostates' to 'electrostates'. China currently dominates global clean energy production, and the US has responded by subsidising the manufacture of batteries and electric vehicles, renewable energy and green hydrogen. In Biden's Washington, a new consensus has emerged that industrial policy is key to national security. Investing in clean energy capacity is considered part and parcel of competing with Beijing for leadership of tomorrow's economy.

Australia has a crucial role to play in this energy transition, including as a major supplier of critical minerals such as lithium, a key component in batteries. Canberra hopes to move up the value chain, from mining to processing critical minerals. More should be done to take advantage of Washington's clean energy subsidies and to incentivise US firms to invest in Australian critical minerals projects.

Australia and the United States can also work together to ensure energy security for countries in our region. An over-concentration of production in China leaves countries vulnerable to supply-chain disruptions, especially as Beijing has shown a willingness to use its market power to coerce other nations into making decisions in its favour. Australia and the US should work with partners to build more resilient and diversified clean energy supply chains in our region: ensuring access to batteries, wind turbines, solar panels and electric vehicles.

Finally, climate change and traditional security concerns are interlinked. Roggeveen says Australia's priority should be ensuring China never establishes bases in the Pacific. For their part, Pacific leaders have repeatedly declared that climate change is their single greatest threat. If Australia wants to cement its place as a security provider of choice in the region, we need to work with Pacific nations to tackle climate change. Australia has put up its hand to host the UN climate talks with Pacific island countries in 2026, which is a good move. But we have to start treating the climate crisis like the emergency that it is.

Wesley Morgan is a senior researcher at the Climate Council, and a research fellow at the Griffith Asia Institute, hosted at Griffith University.

Sam Roggeveen responds

Will Leben's excellent letter urges me to say what I mean, and in that spirit I'll start by acknowledging that he has identified an overstatement in my article. I said the *only* justification for acquiring Tomahawk cruise missiles is to strike the Chinese mainland. But Leben is correct – there are other justifications, such as to strike bases in Australia's neighbourhood.

Still, the best reason to put Tomahawks on nuclear-powered attack submarines (SSNs) is if you want to hit targets really far away. In a behind-the-scenes account of the 2021 meeting in which senior Australian officials first pitched the AUKUS idea to their White House counterparts, journalist Peter Hartcher indicates that this was precisely what the Morrison government had in mind: "My sources didn't put it quite this bluntly, but everyone in the room understood that this was about Australia acquiring the power to pose a direct threat to China's forces and the Chinese mainland."

Luke Gosling and Will Leben both claim to have identified a contradiction in the way I characterise America's role in Asia. It's more like an ambiguity, because right now it simply isn't clear what the United States wants. Leben points to the *CHIPS Act* as a sign of American resolve, but I maintain that the most decisive factor in the regional leadership contest will be military, and the US has clearly not shown enough willingness to win that contest. In the face of China's military modernisation, the largest since World War II, just moving forces around the regional chessboard (Australia, the Philippines and, most recently, Papua New Guinea) won't do.

Gosling cites historical examples to support his claim that the AUKUS submarines won't tie Australia to American military objectives in Asia. We can still behave independently, he insists, just as we did when we brought our troops home in 1942, against Britain's wishes. But as Gosling's colleagues in the parliamentary Labor Party regularly boast, we are entering into a partnership of unprecedented intimacy. AUKUS is entirely novel in Australia's alliance experience, so history isn't much of a guide.

Gosling's assurances also need to be weighed against what the United States believes AUKUS is about. As Kurt Campbell, the Biden administration's lead official on AUKUS, put it in June 2023, "when submarines are provided from the United States to Australia, it's not like they're lost. They will just be deployed by the closest possible allied force." The Americans think AUKUS will buy them a powerful new adjunct to their Pacific fleet. What, and who, could have given them *that* idea?

Contra Gosling, I never said anything about divesting from the US alliance. What I warn about is the consequences of an unprecedented tightening of the alliance, thanks to AUKUS and the new basing arrangements. Sceptics like me are not criticising the alliance as we have known it in our lifetimes, but as something quite new. So it's rather audacious of Gosling to frame the argument as if there are only two choices: support this tightening or support alliance retrenchment.

Let's remind ourselves how we reached this point. Right up until the moment Scott Morrison announced AUKUS on 15 September 2021, support for nuclear-powered submarines existed only on the fringes of Australia's national security debate. No significant Labor figure backed the idea. That AUKUS then instantly became the new orthodoxy says more about our defence debate than it does about my feelings towards the alliance.

I think I understand why Wesley Morgan wants to elevate climate change in security discussions – he wants to broaden the constituency for what he rightly regards as a threat to the planet more urgent than China's military challenge. But is he confident that entrenching this agenda in Australia's security debate, and ultimately inside the security bureaucracy, will produce the results he wants? I fear it won't help the planet, or Australia's defence.

The ADF and other government agencies tasked with ensuring Australia's security are managing zero-sum problems: one nation's security is another's insecurity. Climate change is not that kind of problem. It's a tragedy of the commons, not a security dilemma. Yes, the ADF will have a role in responding to climate-related humanitarian emergencies, but that will never be its core business, because it would require not only a very different force structure but an entirely different identity.

So I'm sceptical about promoting climate change in our security thinking and in the ADF's priorities. In 2013, a former colleague at the Lowy Institute, Linda Jakobson, proposed an Australia-based and Australia-led international centre for humanitarian and disaster relief operations. That's still a good idea. Civil and military forces from around the world could play a part in delivering help around South-East Asia and the Pacific, but this would be a non-military organisation. The core assets for this agency could be the two giant amphibious ships currently operated by our navy: paint them white, with large red crosses, and turn them into floating logistical assets for the region.

Despite my scepticism about nuclear-powered submarines, I don't share Margaret Beavis's concern that AUKUS will open a Pandora's box, encouraging other nations to acquire the same capabilities. To mangle metaphors and commit an atrocious pun, that ship has sailed. Canada was interested in acquiring SSNs well before AUKUS was conceived. Brazil and India have been on this path for a generation or more.

Beavis directs her concerns about nuclear proliferation at the United States and Australia, but I would add a word about China, which since the 1970s has been inexcusably cavalier in its transfer of nuclear and ballistic-missile technology to Pakistan. China is now massively expanding its own nuclear weapons stockpile.

I note this only to raise a final point: nothing I wrote in "Target Australia" should be mistaken for complacency about the scale of the challenge China presents to the regional order, and to Australia's security. I just happen to think Australia is responding to that challenge in strangely counterproductive ways.

Sam Roggeveen is the director of the Lowy Institute's International Security Program and author of The Echidna Strategy: Australia's Search for Power and Peace.

Subscribe to Australian Foreign Affairs & save up to 28% on the cover price.

Forthcoming issue:
Dead in the Water
(February 2024)

Never miss an issue. Subscribe and save.

☐ **1 year auto-renewing print and digital subscription** (3 issues) $49.99 within Australia. Outside Australia $79.99*.

☐ **1 year print and digital subscription** (3 issues) $59.99 within Australia. Outside Australia $99.99.

☐ **1 year auto-renewing digital subscription** (3 issues) $29.99.*

☐ **2 year print and digital subscription** (6 issues) $114.99 within Australia.

☐ **1 year auto-renewing digital Quarterly Essay and Australian Foreign Affairs bundle subscription** (7 issues) $69.99.*

☐ Tick here to commence subscription with the current issue.

Give an inspired gift. Subscribe a friend.

☐ **1 year print and digital gift subscription** (3 issues) $59.99 within Australia. Outside Australia $99.99.

☐ **1 year digital-only gift subscription** (3 issues) $29.99.

☐ **2 year print and digital gift subscription** (6 issues) $114.99 within Australia.

☐ **1 year digital-only Quarterly Essay and Australian Foreign Affairs bundle gift subscription** (7 issues) $69.99.

☐ Tick here to commence subscription with the current issue.

ALL PRICES INCLUDE GST, $11.00 FLAT RATE POSTAGE AUSTRALIA WIDE.

*Your subscription will automatically renew until you notify us to stop. Prior to the end of your subscription period, we will send you a reminder notice.

Please turn over for subscription order form, or subscribe online at **australianforeignaffairs.com**
Alternatively, call 1800 077 514 or +61 3 9486 0288 or email **subscribe@australianforeignaffairs.com**

Back Issues

ALL PRICES INCLUDE GST, $11.00 FLAT RATE POSTAGE AUSTRALIA WIDE.

- ☐ **AFA1** ($19.99)
  The Big Picture
- ☐ **AFA2** ($19.99)
  Trump in Asia
- ☐ **AFA3** ($19.99)
  Australia & Indonesia
- ☐ **AFA4** ($19.99)
  Defending Australia
- ☐ **AFA5** ($19.99)
  Are We Asian Yet?
- ☐ **AFA6** ($19.99)
  Our Sphere of Influence

- ☐ **AFA7** ($19.99)
  China Dependence
- ☐ **AFA8** ($19.99)
  Can We Trust America?
- ☐ **AFA9** ($19.99)
  Spy vs Spy
- ☐ **AFA10** ($19.99)
  Friends, Allies and Enemies
- ☐ **AFA11** ($19.99)
  The March of Autocracy
- ☐ **AFA12** ($19.99)
  Feeling the Heat

- ☐ **AFA13** ($19.99)
  India Rising?
- ☐ **AFA14** ($19.99)
  The Taiwan Choice
- ☐ **AFA15** ($19.99)
  Our Unstable
  Neighbourhood
- ☐ **AFA16** ($19.99)
  The Return of the West
- ☐ **AFA17** ($22.99)
  Girt by China
- ☐ **AFA18** ($22.99)
  We Need to Talk
  About America

PAYMENT DETAILS I enclose a cheque/money order made out to Schwartz Books Pty Ltd.
Or please debit my credit card (MasterCard, Visa or Amex accepted).

CARD NO.

EXPIRY DATE   /   CCV   AMOUNT $

CARDHOLDER'S NAME

SIGNATURE

NAME

ADDRESS

EMAIL   PHONE

Post or fax this form to: Reply Paid 90094, Collingwood VIC 3066 **Freecall:** 1800 077 514 **or** +61 3 9486 0288
Fax: (03) 9011 6106 **Email:** subscribe@australianforeignaffairs.com **Website:** australianforeignaffairs.com
Subscribe online at australianforeignaffairs.com/subscribe (please do not send electronic scans of this form)

The Back Page

LATTICEWORK OF ALLIANCES

What is it: A term to describe the United States' evolving role in Asia, in which Washington supports a network of allies, partners and groupings, as well as their separate relationships.

What it isn't: The approach contrasts with the "hub-and-spoke" model, in which the US was the "hub", connected to allies such as Japan and South Korea. This seventy-year-old model is often credited to John Foster Dulles (secretary of state, US), who once described the US allies in East Asia as "spokes on a wheel".

Who coined it: One of the first figures to use the term was Jake Sullivan (national security advisor, US), who, addressing the Lowy Institute in 2021, called for the US to "build a latticework of alliances and partnerships globally that are … not just about refurbishing the old bilateral alliances".

Who likes it? The Biden administration has presented the latticework model as a departure from the confrontational approach to allies of Donald Trump (former president, US). Charles Edel (Australia Chair, Center for Strategic and International Studies) believes the AUKUS pact between the US, Australia and the United Kingdom exemplifies the model, in which "the United States will play more of a supporting and enabling role for its allies".

Who doesn't? Some observers say the US does not always live up to its latticework aspirations. Susannah Patton (program director, Lowy Institute) has written: "The 'latticework' approach makes sense when the US' goal is to encourage like-minded countries to align with its positions on China. Yet if this comes at the expense of the region's established architecture, it will be at a cost to the US' future influence in Asia."